THE MILITARY HISTORY OF WORLD WAR II
Volume 9

ASIATIC LAND BATTLES:
JAPANESE AMBITIONS
IN THE PACIFIC

The Military History of World War II: Volume 9

ASIATIC LAND BATTLES: JAPANESE AMBITIONS IN THE PACIFIC

by Trevor Nevitt Dupuy
COL., U.S. ARMY, RET.

FRANKLIN WATTS, INC.
575 Lexington Avenue • New York 22

Maps by Dyno Lowenstein

Library of Congress Catalog Card Number: 62-7382
Copyright © 1963 by Franklin Watts, Inc.
Printed in the United States of America

1   2   3   4   5   6   7

Contents

THE MILITARY HISTORY OF WORLD WAR II
Volume 9

ASIATIC LAND BATTLES:
JAPANESE AMBITIONS
IN THE PACIFIC

Japanese Ambitions in the Pacific

The Expanding Empire

IN THE TWENTY YEARS between 1894 and 1914, Japan became the most powerful country in East Asia. Her efficient army and navy crushed China in the Sino-Japanese War of 1894-95, and defeated Russia in the Russo-Japanese War of 1904-5. As a result of these victories Japan gained Formosa, the naval base of Port Arthur on the south coast of Manchuria, and the southern half of the island of Sakhalin. In 1910 she annexed the entire country of Korea.

In 1914 Japan took advantage of the outbreak of World War I in Europe to seize a German-owned seaport on the coast of China and to occupy German colonies spread over the extensive Marshall, Caroline, and Marianas island chains in the Western Pacific. By the end of World War I the Japanese Empire stretched from the ice-bound Kurile Islands to the equator, and from the coast of China to the International Date Line in the mid-Pacific.

The Washington Treaties

THE SUDDEN expansion of the Japanese Empire along the east coast of Asia and into the Central and Southwestern Pacific alarmed those Western nations who had possessions in that part of the world. This was one reason why the United States sponsored the Washington Conference of 1921-22, at which the United States, Great Britain, France, and Japan all agreed to respect each other's rights in their island possessions in the Western Pacific They also agreed not to build any fortifications on these islands. In addition, the United States, Britain, and Japan agreed to limit the size of their navies.

1

Britain, France, and the United States abided by the terms of the Washington Treaties, but Japan did not. She secretly began to fortify the most important of her island posesssions. At the same time, she built more and bigger ships than the Washington Naval Treaty permitted.

Japan was also expanding her influence and control of China. In 1937 this "influence" became a war of conquest, though the Japanese called it "the China Incident." By 1940, Japan had seized most of northeastern China, and all of China's major seaports.

Japanese machine gun nest in China.

The Southern Resources Area

ALTHOUGH JAPAN had become an industrial nation, with many modern factories, she was short of raw materials, and could not produce enough food for her dense population of 70 million people. She could make up these shortages only by trade with other countries. Japanese leaders felt that they must find some sure way of getting essential raw materials in the event of a major war. For this reason, they wanted to get control of the "Southern Resources Area" of southeast Asia, where there were abundant supplies of rice, as well as quantities of nickel, iron, gold, oil, rubber, tin, and many other raw materials.

Most of the territories of this region were colonies belonging to the Western nations: Britain owned Burma, Malaya, and part of Borneo; the remaining East Indies islands belonged to the Netherlands; Indochina was French; the United States owned the Philippines, but had promised independence to the Filipinos by 1946.

Events in Europe in 1940 seemed to provide Japan with an opportunity to conquer those regions she wanted so badly. Nazi Germany, under Adolf Hitler, had conquered France and Holland; Great Britain had lost most of her army, and was desperately preparing for expected Nazi invasions. Russia and the United States were not yet directly affected by the war in Europe, but Russia was busy preparing for war against Germany, and the American Pacific Fleet was much smaller than the Japanese navy. Thus neither Russia nor the United States would be able to interfere seriously with Japanese ambitions.

In September, 1940, Japan began a systematic military occupation of French Indochina, which the French were at that time powerless to resist. At about the same time, Japan signed a ten-year military alliance with Germany and Italy. It was called the "Berlin-Rome-Tokyo Axis."

Victorious Japanese troops atop Nanking walls, December, 1937, cheer their formal occupation of the Chinese city.

In April, 1941, Japan signed a neutrality treaty with Russia. Neither country trusted the other, but neither wanted to fight a war on two fronts. Each could be sure that it would be convenient for the other to abide by this neutrality treaty.

Hoping to get control of the Southern Resources Area without fighting America, Japan carried on diplomatic negotiations with the

4

United States throughout 1941. She was trying to get America to recognize special Japanese rights in the entire Far Eastern region. The United States, for its part, was insisting that Japan must end her war in China, and stop all further military expansion.

In August, 1941, American President Roosevelt warned Japan that further aggression would be met by the United States with "any and all steps necessary." When Japan continued to occupy Indochina, Roosevelt stopped all American trade with Japan. This cut off most of the oil and steel needed by Japanese war industries.

Japan now needed the raw materials of the Southern Resources Area more than ever. America's military forces were still weak, even though they were increasing, and so Japan believed that there would never be a better time than the autumn of 1941 to go to war to get the territories she wanted.

Japan Prepares for War

In October, 1941, therefore, the new Japanese prime minister, General Hideki Tojo, began plans for an early war against the United States. By this time the overall strength of the Japanese army was 2,400,000 men. These were well-equipped soldiers, many with combat experience in China. In addition, Japan had another 3,000,000 trained reserves. Japan's navy and air forces were large, efficient, and ready for war.

In the vast area between American Hawaii and British India, the combined total of the forces of Britain, America, and Holland was 350,000 soldiers, of whom few were well equipped or well trained. The combined air and naval forces of these allies were much smaller than those of Japan, and their ships and planes were older, smaller, and slower.

Outbreak of the Pacific War

Japanese Plans

THE JAPANESE Imperial General Staff carefully prepared a war plan to take full advantage of Japan's overwhelming military superiority in the Far East. First, they intended to seize the Southern Resources Area and additional strategic islands by three principal offensive drives. One of these would begin on the continent of Asia and would be directed against Malaya and Singapore. The second would start soon afterward with a sea invasion of the Philippines. These two drives would then converge against Java, the heart of the Netherlands East Indies. Meanwhile, the Japanese would occupy Thailand as a base for the third offensive — an invasion of Burma. At the outset of the war, smaller forces would quickly seize British Hong Kong and American Guam and Wake Islands.

The Japanese knew that the United States Pacific Fleet, based in Hawaii, would be the only military force that could seriously interfere with their offensives. Therefore the first and most important single operation of the entire initial phase of their war plan was an attack to destroy or neutralize the striking power of the American fleet at Pearl Harbor.

The second phase of the Japanese plan would be a period of consolidation — organizing efficient military control over the conquered territories and establishing a strong defensive ring, or perimeter, around the Japanese Empire. This perimeter would consist of strongholds stretching southward from the Kuriles through Wake Island and the Marshall, Gilbert, and Bismarck island groups, thence westward through northern New Guinea, Timor, and Java, and northward through Sumatra, Malaya, and Burma.

6

The third phase of the Japanese plan would be defensive. The Japanese Imperial General Staff expected to intercept and destroy any Allied attacking force that might attempt to penetrate the defensive perimeter. During this phase they realized that they would be opposed by the full mobilized strength of the United States, which they knew would be much greater than theirs. The Japanese believed, however, that by the time America could mobilize, their own defensive perimeter would be so strong that the Americans would make little progress, and would suffer terrible losses. They felt sure that the prospect of such a long and costly war would so discourage the American people that they would soon be willing to make peace and permit Japan to keep the territories she had seized.

The Japanese Offensives

BY THE BEGINNING of December, the long negotiations in Washington between Japanese envoys and the United States government had reached a deadlock. About this time American, British, and Dutch ships and airplanes reported that Japanese warships and large convoys of troop transports were moving southward from Formosa and from the coast of China into the South China Sea. But no one could tell whether these ships were heading toward southern French Indochina, or toward neutral Thailand — or whether the Japanese were finally about to start the long-expected invasions of British Malaya and the Netherlands East Indies.

There was nothing yet to indicate any Japanese intention to invade the Philippines. Nor was there any hint that the powerful Japanese First Air Fleet, with six large aircraft carriers and other powerful warships, was steaming silently eastward through the cold waters of the north Pacific Ocean with Pearl Harbor as its objective.

7

JAPANESE OFFENSIVES IN THE PACIFIC, DECEMBER 1941

USSR

ALASKA

OUTER MONGOLIA

MANCHUKUO

Sakhalin

KAMCHATKA

KURIL IS.

Attu · Kiska

ALEUTIAN IS.

Peiping ○

CHINA

SHANGHAI

TOKYO

JAPAN

PACIFIC OCEAN

DEC. 7 Pearl Harbor

CHUNGKING

RYUKYU IS.

Okinawa

Bonin Is.

Iwo Jima

Marcus I.

DESTROYER BOMBARDMENT
DEC. 7

Midway Is.

HAWAIIAN IS.

BURMA

FR. INDOCHINA

THAILAND

Hainan

Hong Kong

Formosa

DEC. 23

MARIANA IS

Wake I.
DEC. 8

International Date Line

DEC. 8

MALAYA

PHILIPPINES

DEC. 24

Yap ·

Guam

CAROLINE IS.

Palau Is.

Truk ·

MARSHALL IS.

Palmyra I.

Christmas I.

DEC. 16

Brunei

Borneo

Tarakan DEC. 12

New Guinea

EQUATOR

Singapore

DUTCH EAST INDIES

Sumatra

Java

Celebes

Timor

DARWIN

AUSTRALIA

Bismarck Arch.

Rabaul

Bougainville

SOLOMON IS.

Milne Bay

Tulagi

GILBERT IS

Ellice Is.

Santa Cruz Is.

NEW HEBRIDES

FIJI IS.

Samoa

The initial Japanese operations went exactly according to plan. The blow of Japan's First Air Fleet against Pearl Harbor and other military installations on Oahu was one of the most successful surprise attacks in the long history of warfare. All eight battleships of the American Pacific Fleet were sunk or put out of action for many months. Within a few hours, many thousands of miles further west, other Japanese planes began to strike Malaya, Hong Kong, the Philippines, Guam, and Wake. Amphibious landings began in Thailand and

Honolulu Star-Bulletin 1st EXTRA

8 PAGES— HONOLULU, TERRITORY OF HAWAII, U. S. A., SUNDAY, DECEMBER 7, 1941—8 PAGES ★ PRICE FIVE CENTS

WAR!

(Associated Press by Transpacific Telephone)

SAN FRANCISCO, Dec. 7.—President Roosevelt announced this morning that Japanese planes had attacked Manila and Pearl Harbor.

OAHU BOMBED BY JAPANESE PLANES

SIX KNOWN DEAD, 21 INJURED, AT EMERGENCY HOSPITAL

Attack Made On Island's Defense Areas

By UNITED PRESS

WASHINGTON, Dec. 7. —Text of a White House announcement detailing the attack on the Hawaiian islands is:

"The Japanese attacked Pearl Harbor from the air and all naval and military activities on the island of Oahu, principal American base in the Hawaiian islands."

Oahu was attacked at 7:55 this morning by Japanese planes.

The Rising Sun, emblem of Japan, was seen on plane wing tips.

Wave after wave of bombers streamed through the clouded morning sky from the southwest and flung their missiles on a city resting in peaceful Sabbath calm.

According to an unconfirmed report re-

CIVILIANS ORDERED OFF STREETS

The army has ordered that all civilians stay off the streets and highways and not use telephones.

Evidence that the Japanese attack has registered some hits was shown by three billowing pillars of smoke in the Pearl Harbor and Hickam field area.

All navy personnel and civilian defense workers, with the exception of women, have been ordered to duty at Pearl Harbor.

The Pearl Harbor highway was immediately a mass of racing cars.

A trickling stream of injured people began pouring into the city emergency hospital a few minutes after the bombardment started.

Thousands of telephone calls almost swamped the Mutual Telephone Co., which put extra operators on duty.

At The Star-Bulletin office the phone calls deluged the single operator and it was impossible for this newspaper, for sometime, to handle the flood of calls. Here also an emergency operator was called.

HOUR OF ATTACK—7:55 A. M.

An official army report from department

ANTIAIRCRAFT GUNS IN ACTION

First indication of the raid came shortly before 8 this morning when antiaircraft guns around Pearl Habor began sending up a thunderous barrage.

At the same time a vast cloud of black smoke arose from the naval base and also from Hickam field where flames could be seen.

BOMB NEAR GOVERNOR'S MANSION

Shortly before 9:30 a bomb fell near Washington Place, the residence of the governor. Governor Poindexter and Secretary Charles M. Hite were there.

It was reported that the bomb killed an unidentified Chinese man across the street in front of the Schuman Carriage Co. where windows were broken.

C. E. Daniels, a welder, found a fragment of shell or bomb at South and Queen Sts. which he brought into the City Hall. This fragment weighed about a pound.

At 10:05 a. m. today Governor Poindexter telephoned to The Star-Bulletin announcing he has declared a state of emergency for the entire territory.

He announced that Edouard L. Doty, execu-

Hundreds See City Bombed

Hundreds of Honolulans who hurried to the top of Punchbowl soon after bombs began to fall, saw spread out before them the whole panorama of surprise attack and defense.

Far off over Pearl Harbor the white sky was polka-dotted with anti-aircraft smoke.

Sailing away from the navy base were billowing clouds of tall black smoke from a burst of flame reddened the black sourse of the smoke.

Out from the silver-surfaced mouth of the harbor a flotilla of destroyers streamed in battle formation pouring from their curves

Turn to Page 3, Column 5

Schools Closed

All schools on Oahu, both public and private, will remain closed until further notice, Edward L. Doty, territorial director of civilian defense announced at 11 a.m. today. This does not apply elsewhere

Names of Dead and Injured

The city emergency hospital reported at 10:30 a list of 6 killed and 21 injured.

The complete list will be announced later. Here is a partial list:

Peter Lopes, 34, of 1941 Booanina St., was reported at 9:30 a. m. to be in serious condition from wounds in the lower abdomen.

Herman Gonsalves, of 1702 Kuhio St. is suffering from a mangled thigh, lacerations on the right leg and left arm.

A Portuguese girl, unidentified, 14 years old, died on arrival from previous wounds.

Another victim who died on arrival was Frank Ohashi, M. 1742 Kamamalu St., from punctures wounds in the chest.

Camille Brandli, W. Hawaiian Electric Co. employee, was released from Lunalilo hospital after treatment for lacerations.

Turn to Page 3, Column 5

Malaya, and a land assault was launched against Hong Kong. Japanese naval forces and troop transports were moving toward objectives in the Philippine Islands, and toward Guam and Wake.

The Battles for Wake and Guam

LONELY WAKE ISLAND lies halfway between the Hawaiian and Philippine Islands — more than two thousand miles from each. It was an important link in the chain of American airfields connecting Hawaii with Guam and the Philippines. The capture of Wake, therefore, would isolate the Philippines, while providing the Japanese with a valuable outpost in their Central Pacific perimeter.

In December, 1941, the garrison of Wake consisted of a detachment of 450 Marines, and 12 Marine fighter airplanes. Commanding the Marine detachment on the island was Major James P. S. Deveraux.

During the morning of December 8, Japanese airplanes based on the Marshall Islands began a long-range bombardment of Wake Island that continued for fifteen days. That same day a Japanese naval task force of three light cruisers, six destroyers, and two small troop transports sailed from Kwajelein to capture Wake.

On December 11, Japanese marines attempted to land on Wake under the cover of intense naval gunfire support from the nine warships. But equally intense and accurate fire from the United States Marine defenders sank two Japanese destroyers and repulsed the attackers. The badly damaged Japanese task force limped back to Kwajalein to reorganize, while the aerial bombardment continued. Greatly reinforced, the Japanese returned to Wake on December 23. This time they had air support from two of the carriers that had attacked Pearl Harbor.

The continuing Japanese air assault had severely damaged instal-

Colonel James P. S. Devereux, U.S.M.C.

lations on Wake, and had exhausted the American Marines. Though they had fought bravely, they could not halt the overwhelming Japanese forces that poured across the beaches. Major Devereaux and his men were forced to surrender.

Meanwhile, on December 8, Japanese planes had begun to bombard Guam, the largest island in the Pacific between the Philippines and Hawaii. Guam was garrisoned by five hundred Marines and sailors, but in accordance with the terms of the Washington Treaty, there were no fortifications, no coast defense guns, no antiaircraft guns.

11

On December 10, covered by intense naval gunfire, five thousand Japanese troops stormed onto Guam before dawn. For several hours the lightly armed Americans fought desperately, but they were overwhelmed soon after daybreak.

Probably the only serious mistake the Japanese made at the outset of the war was their failure to capture the American outpost of Midway Island, only eleven hundred miles northwest of Oahu. They could have captured it easily after their great victory at Pearl Harbor, but they contented themselves with a brief after-dark bombardment of Midway by two destroyers on December 7. Things remained quiet at Midway for nearly six months.

The Fall of the Philippines

The Opposing Forces

IN 1934, THE UNITED STATES had promised that on July 4, 1946, it would grant complete independence to the Philippine Islands. Meanwhile, it had established the self-governing Philippine Commonwealth to administer the islands while the Filipinos, with American help, prepared for independence. A small American military garrison remained in the Philippines while the United States assisted the Commonwealth government to establish its own new army. In 1935, the retired American General Douglas MacArthur was invited by the Commonwealth government to organize and train this army.

In 1941, as war clouds gathered over the Far East, President Roosevelt called General MacArthur back to active duty in the American Army. MacArthur was placed in command of the American garrison in the Philippines, as well as of the army of the Philippine

Commonwealth. The Filipino people, under the leadership of their president, Manuel Quezon, were completely loyal to the United States. Unlike many other peoples of southeast Asia, they were not fooled by Japanese propaganda about "Asia for the Asiatics." They had learned that America was a staunch friend.

In December, 1941, MacArthur's force consisted of 13,000 American troops, plus 12,000 excellent Filipino soldiers in the Philippine Scouts of the United States Army. At this time the Philippine Commonwealth Army consisted of about 100,000 men, but these were only partially trained, and they had very little equipment. Air support was provided by the United States Army Air Force, with about 140 first-line aircraft.

The Japanese Fourteenth Army, under Lieutenant General Masaharu Homma, was assigned responsibility for invading the Philippines. With nearly 60,000 combat troops, supported by the powerful Japanese Third Fleet, Homma's first objective was to capture Luzon, the principal island in the Philippines. The Japanese high command expected that this would take about a month and a half.

The Opposing Plans

DURING the 1920's and 1930's, the terms of the Washington Naval Treaty had prevented the United States from strengthening the fortifications of the Philippine Islands. During these years, American military men had known that the defense of the islands against a Japanese invasion would be hopeless. By late 1941, however, under the dynamic leadership of General MacArthur, the Americans and the Filipinos began to feel that their combined forces had some chance of success. In late November, because of the threat of war against Japan, a large convoy of American reinforcements, as well as weapons and equipment for the Philippine Army, had sailed from the west coast of the United States. Several more B-17 "Flying Fortress" bombers were scheduled to arrive in December to join the thirty-five B-17's already in the Philippines. With more reinforcements and supplies promised, MacArthur believed that by mid-1942 he could repulse a Japanese invasion.

Unfortunately, he would not have that much time.

The largest and most important air and ground military installations of the Philippines were located in the central plain of Luzon, north of Manila, the capital. To the west of this city lay the broad expanse of Manila Bay. North of the entrance to the bay was mountainous Bataan Peninsula. To the south, between Bataan and the naval base of Cavite, the entrance to the bay was guarded by precipitous Corregidor Island. Old, but still powerful, coast defenses were located on Corregidor and several small nearby islands.

General Homma's plan was to make his main landing at Lingayen Gulf, on the northwest coast of Luzon, and then to drive southeastward toward Manila. There were about forty-five thousand men in this Japanese landing force. Additional troops would make diversionary landings on the northern and southeastern coasts of the island so that the Americans would have to divide their forces, making it very difficult for them to protect Manila.

The Invasion

BECAUSE of Japan's threatening attitude, American and Filipino forces were alerted for war on November 27, 1941. Air force and antiaircraft units drove off Japanese patrol planes which appeared over the Philippines early on December 8. But about noon, because of lack of proper security precautions at Clark Field, most of the

14

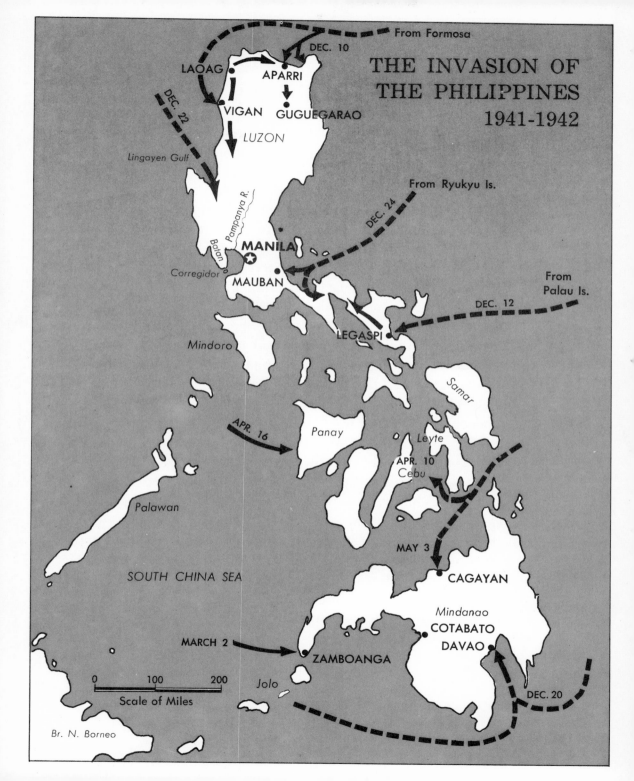

THE INVASION OF
THE PHILIPPINES
1941-1942

From Formosa

DEC. 10

LAOAG
APARRI

DEC. 22

VIGAN
GUGUEGARAO

LUZON

Lingayen Gulf

Pampanya R.

From Ryukyu Is.

DEC. 24

Bataan

MANILA

Corregidor

MAUBAN

From
Palau Is.

DEC. 12

LEGASPI

Mindoro

Samar

APR. 16

Panay

Leyte

APR. 10
Cebu

Palawan

MAY 3

SOUTH CHINA SEA

CAGAYAN

Mindanao
COTABATO
DAVAO

MARCH 2

ZAMBOANGA

Jolo

DEC. 20

0   100   200
Scale of Miles

Br. N. Borneo

American planes were on the ground at their airfields when they were surprised by a massive Japanese bombing attack. About half of the planes were destroyed, and most of the rest were damaged.

On December 10, small Japanese landings were made along the north coast of Luzon. On December 12, another landing was made at Legaspi, near the southeast tip of the island. General MacArthur was certain that these were diversions, so he kept his main army concentrated in central Luzon to meet the main attack.

As MacArthur had expected, the principal Japanese landing was made at Lingayen Gulf, on the western shore of Luzon. On December 22, the invading troops landed under the cover of a tremendous supporting aerial and naval gunfire bombardment of the beaches. They were met at the beaches by MacArthur's Northern Luzon Force, commanded by Major General Jonathan M. Wainwright.

MacArthur had hoped to drive the Japanese back into the sea, but he soon discovered that his inexperienced Filipinos could not stand up against the veteran Japanese. All that saved Wainwright's troops from complete disaster was the effectiveness of the Philippine Scouts 26th Cavalry Regiment and other regular American and Philippine Scout units. Assisted by the heroic defensive efforts of these troops, Wainwright rallied most of his Philippine Army units and began a withdrawal southward to Bataan, as ordered by General MacArthur.

Meanwhile, incessant Japanese bombardments of Manila were causing terrible loss of life and creating panic in the civilian population. For the sake of humanity, therefore, on December 26, MacArthur declared Manila an open city and moved his headquarters to the island of Corregidor. President Quezon, with a few other Philippine Commonwealth government officials, accompanied MacArthur.

Victorious Japanese troops drive into Manila

The Withdrawal to Bataan

THE MOST DIFFICULT part of the withdrawal to Bataan was to get the South Luzon Force, commanded by Major General Albert M. Jones, past Manila and across the broad and marshy Pampanga River Valley before Wainwright's command was driven back to the shores of Manila Bay. Despite confusion and the frequent collapse of the fighting front of the Filipino divisions, the withdrawal was accomplished successfully.

The main credit must go to the courage and determination of the terribly outnumbered, scattered detachments of Wainwright's regular American and Philippine Scout units, who responded magnificently to superb leadership. On December 31, when it seemed as though the South Luzon Force was hopelessly trapped, these exhausted troops launched an amazing counterattack and drove Homma's troops briefly out of the Pampanga Delta.

By dawn of January 1, 1942, the South Luzon Force had withdrawn across the Pampanga River. On January 7, MacArthur's troops held a battle line of nearly twenty miles across the northern portion of the Bataan Peninsula. But in the face of fierce Japanese attacks, it soon became evident that this line was too long to be defended successfully by the shaky Philippine Army troops.

On January 22, under intensive Japanese pressure on both sides of the line, the defenders withdrew southward about eight miles to occupy a new line only twelve miles long, between Bagac and Orion. This line was only fourteen miles north of the tip of the Bataan Peninsula.

Homma now thought that the American defenses were about to crack. During the night of January 23, Japanese troops made amphibious landings along the west coast of the peninsula, intending to drive north to strike the retreating defenders in the rear. To their

18

U.S. and Filipino soldiers mine a bridge on Luzon.

surprise, American and Filipino troops stopped them on the beaches and isolated them on two narrow points of land. During the nights that followed, Homma sent reinforcements, and a new Japanese landing was attempted on the night of January 26. This, too, was stopped on the beach.

On January 27, Homma ordered violent assaults all along the new American defense line from Bagac to Orion. One small penetration, near the center of the line, was quickly contained. All of the other attacks were repulsed.

By now the experience of battle, combined with the splendid leadership of General MacArthur and his American officers, had imparted some steadiness to the Philippine Army soldiers. On February 7, they held their positions while the regular troops counterattacked to eliminate all of the small Japanese beachheads near Mariveles. The American defenses were intact, and the Japanese had suffered a severe defeat.

General Homma had now lost so many men that he knew he could not attack again. On February 8, he asked Tokyo for reinforcements. The Battle of Bataan now settled down to a long period of trench warfare, siege operations.

The defenders of Bataan were completely isolated from the outside world. Filipino and American civilian refugees were eating up food supplies that had originally been intended only for the soldiers. Early in January, General MacArthur had been forced to order half-rations for everyone except the sick and wounded. There were no Allied forces available to break the blockade or to send reinforcements to MacArthur. Only small quantities of a few special supplies reached Corregidor and Bataan by submarine. The American government in Washington, and General MacArthur on Corregidor, knew that defeat in the Philippines was inevitable.

The important thing was for the troops on Bataan to hold out as long as they could, in order to delay the Japanese offensives and to permit the United States and her allies to complete the hasty measures they were taking to save Australia from a possible invasion. The few available American troops were being rushed to Hawaii to strengthen that outpost and to garrison islands along the air-ferry route across the South Pacific to Australia and New Zealand. A newly created and only partially trained American division was sent to garrison the French island of New Caledonia. American and Australian bomber and fighter planes were rushed to northern Australia and to outposts on the large island of New Guinea.

Departure of General MacArthur

IN FEBRUARY, General MacArthur was instructed by the American War Department to leave the Philippines and go to Australia. His experience and ability were needed to command Allied forces in that area. At first he refused to go, but on February 23, President Roosevelt personally repeated the order.

On the night of March 12, MacArthur reluctantly left Corregidor with his family and a few staff officers on some American PT (motor-torpedo) boats. He appointed General Wainwright in command in the Philippines. Wainwright moved to Corregidor, leaving Major General Edward P. King to command on Bataan.

Meanwhile, MacArthur's party arrived at Mindanao and transferred to B-17 bombers, which flew them to Port Darwin in Australia. Upon his arrival there, on March 16, General MacArthur broadcast a promise to the Filipino people, to his troops still holding the line at Bataan — and to the Japanese:

"I shall return."

BATAAN AND CORREGIDOR

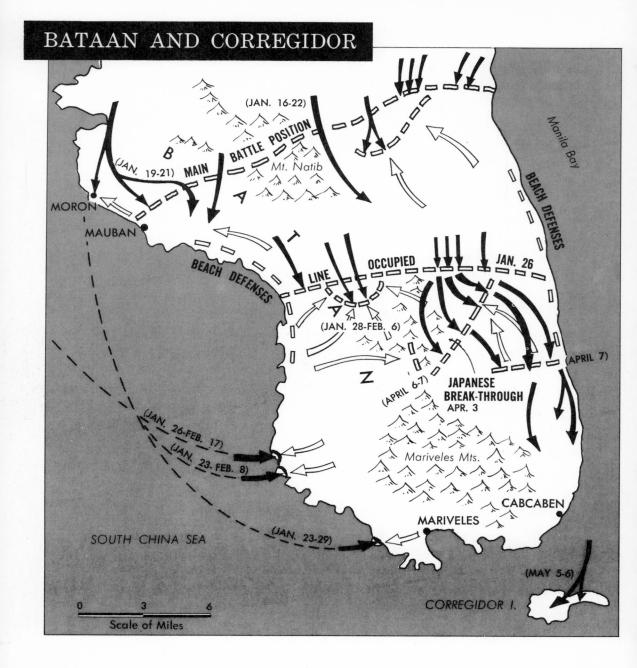

(JAN. 16-22)

B

(JAN. 19-21) MAIN BATTLE POSITION

Mt. Natib

A

MORON

MAUBAN

BEACH DEFENSES

Manila Bay

BEACH DEFENSES

I

LINE OCCUPIED

JAN. 26

A

(JAN. 28-FEB. 6)

Z

(APRIL 6-7)

(APRIL 7)

JAPANESE BREAK-THROUGH APR. 3

(JAN. 26-FEB. 17)

(JAN. 23-FEB. 8)

Mariveles Mts.

CABCABEN

MARIVELES

(JAN. 23-29)

SOUTH CHINA SEA

0   3   6
Scale of Miles

(MAY 5-6)

CORREGIDOR I.

The Fall of Bataan

GENERAL HOMMA now began to increase pressure against the American-Filipino defense lines. He knew that the defenders had been on half-rations for almost three months, and were now seriously weakened by shortage of food. On April 1 this reduced ration was again cut in half, as Wainwright tried to preserve his dwindling supplies.

The Japanese launched their final attack on April 3, under the cover of overwhelming air and artillery bombardment. The well-trained, well-fed Japanese quickly broke through the defending lines. Though the exhausted, starving Filipinos and Americans fought bravely, they were unable to stem the Japanese advance. On April 9, General King and the remnants of the defenders of Bataan were forced to surrender.

Then occurred one of the greatest tragedies of the war. The Japanese had only contempt for their own soldiers who surrendered, and so they were equally contemptuous of captured enemies, and generally treated them badly. Brutally and ruthlessly they forced the exhausted Allied survivors of the Battle of Bataan to march in blazing heat to prisons in Manila. Hundreds died on this "Death March," and thousands more died as a result of this and later mistreatment. This was one of a number of similar black marks to hold against an otherwise worthy and courageous enemy.

The Defense of Corregidor

DURING the remainder of April and the early days of May, Japanese airplanes rained bombs incessantly on Corregidor and on the small forts in the mouth of Manila Bay. They lined the southern tip of the Bataan Peninsula with their heavy guns, and hammered at these last

Bataan Death March.

American strongholds. The guns on the islands fired back accurately and effectively, but one by one the American batteries were knocked out by the overwhelmingly superior Japanese air and artillery units.

Soon after dark on the night of May 5, Japanese troops landed on the northeastern tip of Corregidor. They started to advance inland but were thrown back to the beaches by counterattacks. More boats, carrying reinforcements, arrived, but many of these were smashed by point-blank American artillery and machine-gun fire. The slaughter of the Japanese literally sickened the defending troops.

By dawn the Japanese were beginning to advance again from their beachhead. Telephone communications had been disrupted on the island, the water supply had been cut. The American artillery had been knocked out; all American and Filipino troops were now en-

Aerial view of Corregidor Island.

A Japanese officer on Mindanao holds the Naval Ensign.

gaged in the fighting, so there were no reserves to meet new assault forces coming across the bay. By noon General Wainwright realized that he could do no more damage to the Japanese, and so, in order to save further loss of life, he surrendered his command to General Homma.

Many American and Filipino troops took to the mountain jungles throughout the Philippines and kept up continuous guerrilla war against the Japanese for two and a half years. But most of the islands were soon under effective Japanese control.

The Japanese had expected to conquer the Philippines in fifty days. It took them three times that long. There were two principal reasons for this. First was the strategical and tactical superiority of General MacArthur over his opponent, General Homma. Second was the magnificent conduct of the defending troops. Time and again the Philippine Scouts proved that they were more than a match for the best in the Japanese army. And after their early and almost disastrous baptism of fire, the troops of the Philippine Army performed almost as well. The few American units in the islands fought with a gallantry never exceeded in American military history. American artillery was particularly efficient. Starvation, disease, and sheer physical exhaustion had reduced the stamina of the defending troops to the vanishing point before they were defeated.

Holding the Line in the Pacific

Allied Reorganization

EARLY IN 1942 President Roosevelt and Prime Minister Churchill established a military command organization to direct the wars against Germany and Japan. They agreed that overall strategic decisions were to be made by the top military leaders of the United States and Great Britain. These generals and admirals, who met frequently to work out and approve plans, called themselves the Combined Chiefs of Staff. The four American members of this committee were called Joint Chiefs of Staff; the three British members were the British Chiefs of Staff Committee. Supervision of all military operations in the Pacific Ocean areas, was assigned the American Joint Chiefs of Staff. Allied naval operations in the Indian Ocean and land operations in Burma, Malaya, and Sumatra were to be supervised by the British Chiefs of Staff.

In the Pacific, the Combined Chiefs of Staff established two principal Allied military organizations. The Southwest Pacific area, commanded by General MacArthur, included Australia, New Guinea, most of the Netherlands East Indies, and the Philippines. The forces in this region were mostly American and Australian.

All other Pacific regions were included in the Pacific Ocean areas, commanded by American Admiral Chester W. Nimitz. Most of Nimitz' forces would be Americans. His area of responsibility was divided into three portions. That north of the 42nd parallel was called the North Pacific area. The region east of Australia, and south of the equator — including the eastern Solomon Islands and New Caledonia — was called the South Pacific area; this was controlled by Vice Admiral Robert L. Ghormley, under the overall command of Admiral Nimitz. The remaining islands, including the Hawaiian Islands and most of the Japanese island groups, made up the Central Pacific area, under Nimitz' direct command.

Both General MacArthur and Admiral Ghormley had been assigned the mission of checking further Japanese advances in their areas, but because of the demands of the war in Europe, only limited

Allied forces were available to them. With these forces, however, they were ordered to carry out limited counterattacks to weaken the Japanese and to prepare for later large-scale offensives against Japan, once Germany was defeated.

The Japanese Try More Conquests

ALTHOUGH the Japanese had been unexpectedly delayed in the Philippines, all other parts of the first phase of their plan had gone more rapidly and more successfully than they had expected. Between January 11 and February 28 they had made numerous amphibious and airborne landings on the major islands of the Netherlands East Indies, and had forced the Dutch to surrender on March 9.

Instead of following the second phase of their plan, and simply strengthening and consolidating the defensive perimeter that they had conquered, the Japanese now decided to extend this perimeter to the eastward and to the southeastward. They decided to seize outposts in the Aleutian Islands and to capture the island of Midway, in the Central Pacific, as well as Papua (southeastern New Guinea), and the Solomon Islands in the Southwest Pacific.

The first step in this new Japanese plan was to send amphibious task forces to seize bases in the southeastern Solomon Islands and in the Louisiade Archipelago, and to capture Port Moresby in southern Papua. American naval forces attacked these convoys, and this led to the air and naval Battle of the Coral Sea, on May 7 and 8, 1942. The battle was indecisive, but the Japanese convoys heading for Port Moresby and the Louisiade Islands turned back. They did, however, establish an outpost on Tulagi Island in the southeastern Solomons.

Less than a month later, Admiral Isoroku Yamamoto led the main

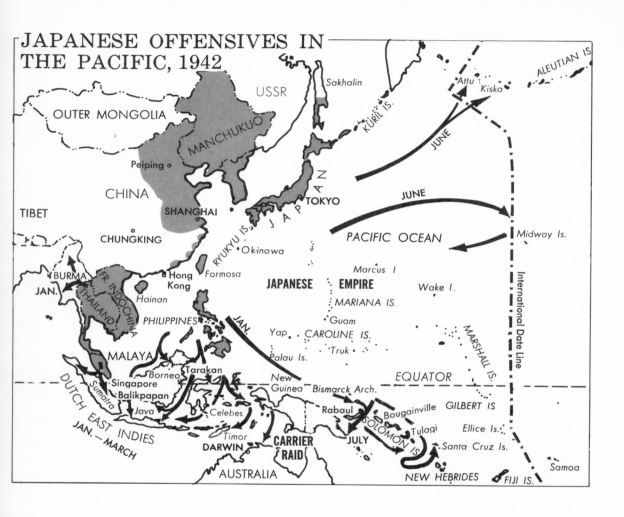

JAPANESE OFFENSIVES IN
THE PACIFIC, 1942

OUTER MONGOLIA

USSR

Sakhalin

ALEUTIAN IS

Attu

Kiska

MANCHUKUO

KURIL IS.

JUNE

Peiping o

CHINA

TOKYO

JUNE

TIBET

SHANGHAI

PACIFIC OCEAN

Midway Is.

CHUNGKING

RYUKYU IS.

Okinawa

Marcus I

JAPANESE   EMPIRE

Wake I.

BURMA

FR. INDOCHINA

Formosa

Hong
Kong

MARIANA IS.

JAN.

THAILAND

Hainan

Guam

Yap ·

CAROLINE IS.

MARSHALL IS.

International Date Line

PHILIPPINES

JAN.

Truk

MALAYA

Palau Is.

Singapore

Borneo

Tarakan

New
Guinea

EQUATOR

Balikpapan

Bismarck Arch.

GILBERT IS

Sumatra

Java

Celebes

Rabaul

Bougainville

DUTCH

Timor

Tulagi

Ellice Is.

EAST

DARWIN

CARRIER
RAID

JULY

SOLOMON IS.

Santa Cruz Is.

INDIES

JAN. — MARCH

AUSTRALIA

NEW HEBRIDES

FIJI IS.

Samoa

Japanese fleet and a large convoy of troop transports toward Midway. At the same time, a smaller Japanese amphibious force sailed for the Aleutian Islands. The naval Battle of Midway began on June 3. The main forces of the Japanese and American fleets never sighted each other; the battle was fought at long range between the carriers and their airplanes. By June 6, the Japanese had suffered a crushing defeat at the hands of the small American fleet, and the expedition to Midway was abandoned. The Japanese succeeded, however, in establishing footholds on the Aleutian islands of Attu and Kiska.

Damage done on Midway Island before the Japanese were beaten off.

The defeat at Midway caused the Japanese to give up their plans for extending their defensive perimeter. They now decided that its southeastern portion would be anchored by naval and air bases at Rabaul, in New Britain, with outposts on the island of Guadalcanal, in the southern Solomons, and on Port Moresby. In Papua, they immediately sent an expedition overland from Buna across the Owen Stanley Mountains to seize Port Moresby.

The Papuan Campaign

THUS, before General MacArthur could start his planned limited offensives, he was forced to fight a desperate defensive battle for Port Moresby. In August, Australian units attempting to delay the Japanese advance were driven southward over the Owen Stanley Mountains. At the same time, another Japanese force made an amphibious landing at Milne Bay on the eastern tip of New Guinea. But now, with excellent support from American and Australian planes, the Australian soldiers struck back. A counterattack at Milne Bay defeated the invaders, and remnants were evacuated by Japanese destroyers. Simultaneously, the Australian 7th Division halted the Japanese main advance at Kokoda, only thirty miles from Port Moresby. Then, in early September, the Australians counterattacked.

Slowly, in bitter fighting, the Japanese were pushed back across the mountains. At the same time, MacArthur sent American troops by sea and air to establish a base on the east coast of Papua, near Buna. By mid-November these combined movements had forced the Japanese to withdraw to strongly fortified coastal positions between Gona and Buna. Here they had established a line of bunkers — trenches and dugouts covered with heavy logs and sandbags, under mounds of earth screened by fast-growing vegetation. These bunkers contained numerous machine guns, and were covered by fire from well-protected and well-concealed artillery positions.

The Allied troops gradually surrounded this powerful stronghold, but the Australians were exhausted by their extended mountain fighting and marching, and the Americans were entirely inexperienced in jungle warfare. The Allies were also short of rations and ammunition. After six weeks of inconclusive fighting, the Japanese still held all their main positions, while disease and casualties had cut the attacking force almost in half.

General MacArthur then sent Lieutenant General Robert L. Eichelberger to take command of Allied forces near Buna and Gona. By personal initiative and leadership Eichelberger rallied the demoralized Allied troops. When reinforcements finally arrived, he began a slow but steady advance that drove the Japanese back into an ever-shrinking perimeter. The Japanese fiercely contested every foot of ground, and losses were high on both sides. The Allied forces captured Gona on December 9. In January they stormed Buna. By January 22, 1943, they had wiped out all Japanese resistance in the area.

Guadalcanal Campaign

ADMIRAL GHORMLEY had been ordered to seize the southeastern Solomons even before anyone knew that the Japanese were building up a stronghold on Guadalcanal. When the Joint Chiefs of Staff realized what the Japanese were doing, they ordered Ghormley to rush preparations for his offensive. His first objective was now to be the seizure of the newly established Japanese airfield on the northern shore of Guadalcanal.

The principal ground force element of Ghormley's Amphibious Force was the 1st Marine Division, commanded by Major General

Marines land on Guadalcanal. November, 1942.

Alexander A. Vandegrift. Though they had seen no previous combat action in the war, these were tough, veteran troops, trained for amphibious operations and jungle warfare.

On August 7, 1942, Marine landing forces went ashore on the northern coast of Guadalcanal and on the nearby islands of Florida

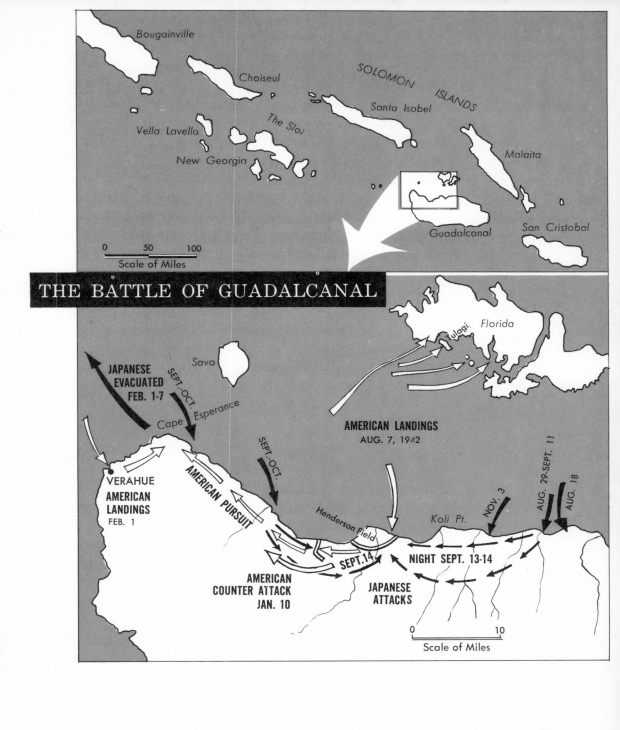

Bougainville

Choiseul

SOLOMON ISLANDS

Santa Isabel

Vella Lavella

The Slot

New Georgia

Malaita

San Cristobal

Guadalcanal

0   50   100
Scale of Miles

THE BATTLE OF GUADALCANAL

Tulagi   Florida

Savo

JAPANESE EVACUATED FEB. 1-7

SEPT.-OCT.

Cape Esperance

SEPT.-OCT.

AMERICAN LANDINGS
AUG. 7, 1942

VERAHUE
AMERICAN LANDINGS
FEB. 1

AMERICAN PURSUIT

Henderson Field

Koli Pt.

NOV. 3

AUG. 29-SEPT. 11

AUG. 18

SEPT. 14

NIGHT SEPT. 13-14

AMERICAN COUNTER ATTACK JAN. 10

JAPANESE ATTACKS

0   10
Scale of Miles

and Tulagi. A sharp fight took place on Tulagi before the Marines seized control of the hills dominating the anchorage between Tulagi and Florida. There was almost no opposition on Guadalcanal. By the evening of August 7, the Marines had driven the surprised Japanese from the airfield and had established a defensive perimeter against the expected Japanese counterattack.

This came soon, but in a manner that caught the American naval escorting fleet completely by surprise. Undetected by the Americans, a Japanese naval squadron slipped past Savo Island during the night of August 8-9. It sank four Allied cruisers in a few minutes, then escaped unharmed.

The Allied defeat at the Battle of Savo Island, combined with intensive Japanese aerial attacks from Rabaul, persuaded Admiral

Japanese pagoda used as headquarters for U.S. Marine and Navy fliers at Henderson Field, Guadalcanal.

Ghormley to withdraw the naval covering forces and supply transports from the waters near Guadalcanal. The 1st Marine Division suddenly found itself isolated in its small perimeter around newly named Henderson Field.

Japanese planes now began a series of bombing and strafing attacks which would continue for many weeks to come. At the same time, Japanese warships and transports began rushing southeastward through the Solomon Islands from Rabaul, carrying reinforcements to Guadalcanal. As their strength built up, veteran Japanese jungle fighters began to harass the Marines' defense perimeter.

The first organized Japanese ground attacks on Guadalcanal began on August 17, but the Marines repulsed them easily. In the following days "the Tokyo Express" brought more Japanese troops ashore, and the assaults were repeated. A serious battle took place from September 12 to September 14 as the Japanese tried to capture positions on Lunga Ridge, overlooking Henderson Field from the south. They came close to breaking the Marines' lines in this Battle of the Ridge, but they were finally repulsed.

During the following weeks the Japanese continued to rush soldiers to Guadalcanal by single ship and by convoy. The American Navy, as well as Army, Marine, and Navy airplanes, struck back to try to prevent the arrival of these reinforcements. But night after night, Japanese vessels steamed through "the Slot" — an inside passage between the islands of New Georgia and Santa Isabel — to land more troops, and to bombard the Marine positions around Henderson Field.

Meanwhile, American Marine and Army reinforcements were also arriving at Guadalcanal. By the middle of October, the strength of each side had been built up to over twenty thousand men.

On October 23, General Hyakutake's Seventeenth Army launched a two-division attack against the American position. At the same

On Guadalcanal. October, 1942. U.S. Marines advance over a bridge built by Marine Corps engineers.

time a Japanese fleet moved down to prevent the arrival of more American reinforcements. For forty-eight hours the land battle raged before the Japanese finally admitted failure.

The Marines now began to advance from their perimeter, driving the Japanese westward along the north coast of the island. The Japanese made one naval effort to reinforce their ground troops on the island, but it was halted by the American Navy in mid-November as a result of the hard-fought naval Battle of Guadalcanal. Many Japanese troop transports were sunk, with terrible loss of life. Only a few survivors reached the island.

In December, the arrival of American Army and Marine reinforcements permitted the tired 1st Marine Division to withdraw and rest.

A sunken Japanese troop transport ship protrudes bow-high on the beach at Guadalcanal.

The new units, combined into the XIV Corps, began a full-scale offensive in late December. By the end of January, 1943, the Japanese had been completely defeated, and gave up all further efforts to hold the island. Japanese destroyers slipped in at night and evacuated about 13,000 survivors between February 6 and 9. Approximately 25,000 more had been killed in battle, or had been drowned trying to reach the island, while at least 15,000 died of disease or starved. American losses were 1,700 killed and almost 5,000 wounded; most of these casualties were among the Marines.

Converging on Rabaul

The Opposing Plans

BY THE BEGINNING of 1943 the Japanese, realizing that their defensive perimeter was threatened by the American successes on Guadalcanal and in Papua, began to strengthen Rabaul. This was the southeastern anchor of a new perimeter, with outposts on the Huon Gulf in eastern New Guinea and on New Georgia Island in the Solomons.

On the Allied side, General MacArthur was given responsibility for breaking through the new Japanese perimeter. He decided to do this with two converging offensive thrusts. The western drive was to be undertaken by the Sixth Army, commanded by Lieutenant General Walter Krueger, whose mission was to advance along the east coast of New Guinea and to cross the Vitiaz Strait to New Britain. The eastern advance was to be conducted by Admiral William F. Halsey, commander of the South Pacific area and of the American Third Fleet. Halsey's forces, which had been shifted from the control of Nimitz in order to help MacArthur operate against Rabaul, were to advance through the Solomons toward New Britain.

Thanks to the tremendous production of American factories and shipyards, planes and ships were beginning to arrive steadily in the South and Southwest Pacific areas. General MacArthur and his two subordinate commanders were therefore able to gain local air superiority and then, with powerful naval and air support, to land their troops wherever they wanted. MacArthur's strategy was to strike where the Japanese ground strength was weakest, so as to save as many lives as possible. He usually bypassed enemy defensive positions, leaving most of the Japanese land forces in pockets from which they could not break out because of Allied air and naval superiority.

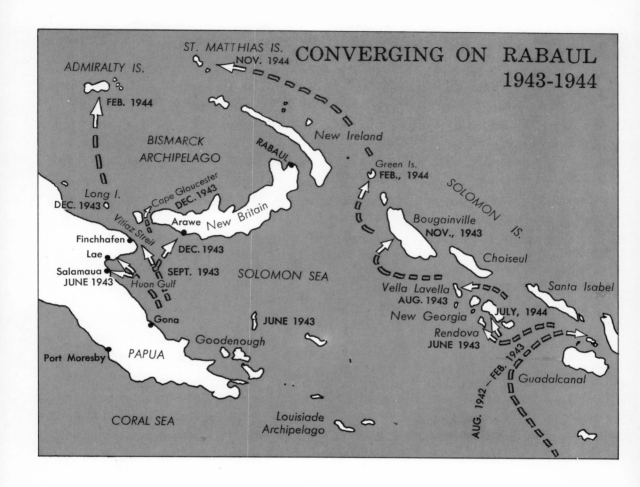

CONVERGING ON RABAUL 1943-1944

ST. MATTHIAS IS.
NOV. 1944

ADMIRALTY IS.

FEB. 1944

New Ireland

BISMARCK
ARCHIPELAGO

RABAUL

Green Is.
FEB., 1944

SOLOMON IS.

Long I.
DEC. 1943

Cape Gloucester
DEC. 1943

Bougainville
NOV., 1943

Vitiaz Strait

Arawe New Britain

Choiseul

Finchhafen

DEC. 1943

Santa Isabel

Lae

SEPT. 1943

SOLOMON SEA

Vella Lavella
AUG. 1943

Salamaua
JUNE 1943

Huon Gulf

JULY, 1944

New Georgia

Gona

JUNE 1943

Rendova
JUNE 1943

Port Moresby

PAPUA

Goodenough

AUG. 1942 – FEB. 1943

Guadalcanal

CORAL SEA

Louisiade
Archipelago

New Guinea and New Britain

GENERAL KRUEGER's offensive in New Guinea could not begin until sufficient supplies had been collected to support the advance, and enough landing craft and air transports were available to permit large-scale amphibious and airborne operations. Meanwhile, the Allies established airfields near Buna and Wau.

Late in June, 1943, Allied forces landed south of Salamaua, on the Huon Gulf. In July and August, American and Australian troops converged on Salamaua. Then, on September 14, while the Japanese were concentrating their attention on these attacks, the Australian 9th Division made an amphibious landing near Lae. At the same time, American airborne troops dropped to seize Nadzab, north of Lae. The Japanese were thrown into confusion, and the Allies captured both Lae and Salamaua in mid-September.

Immediately some of MacArthur's troops advanced overland toward Finschhafen, at the tip of the Huon Peninsula. On September 22, the Marines made an amphibious landing north of the town. The Allies captured Finschhafen on October 20. Most of the key points of the Huon Peninsula were in Allied hands by November.

On December 15, an American Army regiment crossed Vitiaz Strait to make an amphibious landing at Arawe in southern New Britain. Eleven days later, the 1st Marine Division landed on the western tip of New Britain to seize an important airfield at Cape Gloucester. In the next three months the combined Army and Marine forces drove the stubborn Japanese from all of western New Britain.

Through the Solomons

MEANWHILE, on June 30, 1943, in accordance with plans worked out jointly between General MacArthur and Admiral Halsey, troops of

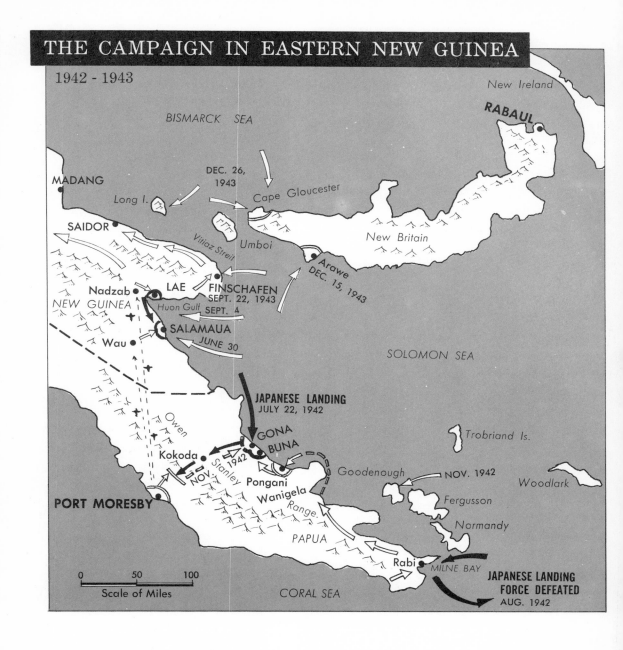

THE CAMPAIGN IN EASTERN NEW GUINEA

1942 - 1943

New Ireland

RABAUL

BISMARCK SEA

MADANG

DEC. 26, 1943

Long I.

Cape Gloucester

New Britain

SAIDOR

Vitiaz Strait

Umboi

Nadzab

LAE

NEW GUINEA

FINSCHAFEN
SEPT. 22, 1943
SEPT. 4

Arawe
DEC. 15, 1943

Huon Gulf

Wau

SALAMAUA

JUNE 30

SOLOMON SEA

Owen

JAPANESE LANDING
JULY 22, 1942

GONA

BUNA

Kokoda

Stanley

NOV. 1942

Pongani

Wanigela

Range.

Trobriand Is.

Goodenough

NOV. 1942

Woodlark

Fergusson

PORT MORESBY

PAPUA

Normandy

Rabi

MILNE BAY

JAPANESE LANDING
FORCE DEFEATED
AUG. 1942

0   50   100

Scale of Miles

CORAL SEA

the XIV Corps landed on the island of Rendova in the central Solomons. This was the first move in an attack to seize Munda, on the Japanese stronghold of New Georgia. In August, while a series of fierce naval battles raged in the waters around New Georgia, the Americans captured Munda, where they established a base for further advance.

On August 15, Halsey bypassed the strong Japanese garrison on the island of Kolombangara to land his troops on Vella Lavella. The Japanese fought fanatically, and it took the American troops until October 9 to capture the island.

To deceive the Japanese, he made a diversionary landing on Choiseul on October 27. As a result, the Japanese were completely surprised when, on November 1, the Americans made their main landing at Empress Augusta Bay, on Bougainville. Before the end of the month, the American troops had cleared the area around the bay. They established a defensive perimeter to protect a new American naval base and three newly constructed airfields that were within fighter range of the main Japanese stronghold at Rabaul, only 235 miles away.

The Allies made no effort at that time to attack the remaining Japanese forces either on Bougainville or elsewhere in the Solomons.

Halsey's next major objective was the large island of Bougainville. Allied planes kept a close watch over them, and American naval and air forces conducted gunnery and bombardment training by attacks against the principal Japanese installations. With neither air nor naval support, these bypassed Japanese troops were helpless. They could do nothing more than to try to survive by gathering food from the jungle.

The Allied tactics of bypassing and isolating large Japanese forces were so successful in eastern New Guinea and in the Solomons that General MacArthur and the Joint Chiefs of Staff now decided that it would be unnecessary to make a costly attack on the Japanese for-

American tank on Bougainville. As the tank advances, infantrymen follow in its cover. The man in front is running to a new position while the tank covers him from direct enemy fire.

SIGNAL CORPS PHOTO

Gun, after a direct hit by a Japanese bomb while the crew was manning it.

tress of Rabaul. By the end of 1943, therefore, General MacArthur was preparing his forces for further advances along the northern coast of New Guinea.

The Central Pacific in 1943 and 1944

Admiral Nimitz' Mission

ADMIRAL NIMITZ was ordered by the Joint Chiefs of Staff to strike west from Hawaii through the Japanese island chains of the Marshalls, Carolines, and the Marianas. The spearheads of this drive through the Central Pacific were expected to meet with those of General MacArthur in the Philippines, or at Formosa, or on the coast of China.

The principal force available to Admiral Nimitz for his westward offensives was the rebuilt Pacific Fleet, with its increasingly effective carrier task forces. Also available to him were the Marines who had been operating under Admiral Halsey and General MacArthur in the South and Southwest Pacific, and new Marine divisions that were being trained in the United States. In addition, several new Army divisions were beginning to arrive in Hawaii.

The left flank of Nimitz' advance through the vast reaches of the Pacific Ocean was protected by General MacArthur's operations in the Southwest Pacific. His north flank was exposed, however, to interference from the Japanese-held islands of Attu and Kiska. The forces holding these fog-shrouded Aleutian islands were not large. However, Kiska and Attu could serve the Japanese as useful bases for hit-and-run air and naval raids against American forces in the

Central Pacific, or against the west coasts of the United States and Canada.

In May, 1943, an amphibious task force under Admiral Thomas C. Kinkaid assaulted Attu. The principal element of this force was the 7th Infantry Division. After an eighteen-day battle, 2,500 Japanese were killed, and 29 prisoners were taken. American casualties were 561 killed and 1,136 wounded.

The Japanese now realized that Kiska was next on the American timetable. On July 29, 1943, a small Japanese naval force secretly and skillfully embarked the 5,400 troops on Kiska and took them back to Japan. The fog was so heavy that American reconnaissance

Aerial view of Attu Island in the Aleutians.

FROM LEATHERNECK

planes and vessels were completely unaware of what the Japanese had done. When American and Canadian troops landed on the island on August 15, they were surprised to find the island deserted.

By this time the Japanese had lost so many warships and airplanes that they decided to reduce the length of their defensive perimeter. The new line extended south from the Kuriles, through the Bonins, Marianas, and Carolines to western New Guinea and Timor, thence westward through the Netherlands East Indies and Malaya to Burma. Outposts east of this line were ordered to hold on as long as possible, but they knew that they would receive no assistance from the Japanese fleet. While these outposts delayed the American advance, the Japanese hoped to gain enough time to rebuild their navy and air forces. Then they planned to strike powerful counteroffensive blows when the Americans began to assault the new perimeter.

Tarawa

ADMIRAL NIMITZ decided to start his advance by invading the Gilbert Islands. The landings were to be made on the islands of Tarawa and Makin. Though his forces were still small, Nimitz knew that the Japanese were fully occupied by General MacArthur's offensives against Rabaul. The amphibious force for this operation was commanded by Rear Admiral Richmond K. Turner. The V Marine Amphibious Corps, commanded by Major General Holland M. Smith, was assigned to make the actual landings.

There were 2,800 Japanese soldiers and 2,000 armed civilian laborers on Tarawa. Makin was occupied by a garrison of 260, with over 500 civilian laborers. During November, the islands were bombarded heavily by American Army, Navy, and Marine Corps planes. Shortly after mid-November, American naval ships added their gunfire to this air hammering.

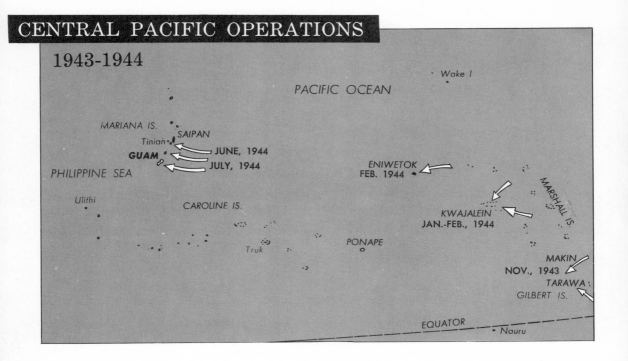

CENTRAL PACIFIC OPERATIONS

1943-1944

PACIFIC OCEAN

Wake I

MARIANA IS.
SAIPAN
Tinian
GUAM — JUNE, 1944
— JULY, 1944

PHILIPPINE SEA

Ulithi

CAROLINE IS.

Truk

PONAPE

ENIWETOK
FEB. 1944

KWAJALEIN
JAN.-FEB., 1944

MARSHALL IS.

MAKIN
NOV., 1943
TARAWA
GILBERT IS.

EQUATOR
Nauru

The landings began on November 21. By the evening of the 23rd, the Army regiment attacking Makin overwhelmed the last Japanese resistance and captured the island. About 100 prisoners, mostly Korean laborers, were taken; some 700 Japanese soldiers and laborers were killed. The Americans lost 66 killed and 152 wounded.

The 2nd Marine Division encountered much more serious Japanese resistance at Tarawa. The island's defenses were extremely strong; the defenders were tough veteran troops. The Marine attackers soon discovered that Japanese artillery and machine guns defend-

U.S. infantry assault Butaritari, Makin Atoll, in the Gilbert Islands.

ing the beaches had not been seriously damaged by the pre-assault bombardment. To make matters worse, the water clearance over the coral reef in front of the beaches was less than had been expected. Many landing craft were stranded on the reef, where they were pounded to pieces by accurate Japanese artillery fire. The Marines discovered that the laborers fought almost as fiercely as the regular Japanese soldiers.

51

On Tarawa a squad leader points out the spot from which the Japanese are firing, and the Marines crawl up on their stomachs to get them.

Here, as in all of the later operations in the Central Pacific, the Japanese were concentrated in a small, heavily fortified area, protected with mines and beach obstacles. On these small islands the American assault troops had no choice but to go ashore on the beaches where the enemy was waiting for them. There was no way that they could avoid intense crossfire from carefully placed and well-protected artillery and machine guns. The Japanese could be dislodged only by shattering air and naval bombardment, followed by hand-to-hand infantry assault.

For twenty-four hours the issue was in doubt. The Marines suffered terrible losses, and were unable to penetrate more than a few yards from the water's edge at any point along the beaches. With grim determination, nevertheless, they continued their assault. Finally, after four days of the most intensive fighting, they wiped out all organized resistance. Only about 150 prisoners, almost all laborers,

Grim-faced, a wounded Marine leader guides his men through a barbed wire entanglement on Tarawa.

A Marine and his buddy (with hand grenade) wait to go over the top on Tarawa. November, 1943.

were taken. The remaining 4,650 Japanese were killed. The Marines lost almost 1,000 killed and over 2,000 wounded.

Tarawa had been a very costly fight. But it taught the Allies some valuable lessons.

The Marshalls

ADMIRAL NIMITZ and his forces now began to prepare for an advance through the Marshall Islands. Kwajalein was their first objective. General Smith's V Marine Amphibious Corps was again given the mission of making the landing. This time the assault troops were the 4th Marine Division, and the Army's 7th Infantry Division, veterans of Attu. The total strength of the assault force was 42,000; the Japanese defenders numbered more than 8,000.

On January 29, 1944, Nimitz' forces began an intensive aerial and naval bombardment against the small group of coral islands which made up Kwajalein Atoll. Two days later the Army troops attacked Kwajalein Island itself, while the Marines landed on the beaches of the heavily fortified northern islands of Namur and Roi. The lessons learned at Tarawa were put to good use. The attacking troops were able to get well past the beaches before they encountered Japanese resistance.

The Japanese did not give up easily, however; the fighting raged for over a week on the islands of the atoll. But by February 8 all resistance had ceased, the fanatical defenders having been killed almost to a man. The Americans lost 1,500 men killed and wounded.

Marines, on the lookout for Japanese snipers, move up on the Marshall Islands.

Admiral Nimitz' next objective was the atoll of Eniwetok, almost 400 miles northwest of Kwajalein. The atoll was defended by a garrison of 3,400 men. A combined landing force of Army and Marine units, totaling nearly 8,000 men, landed there on February 19. The defenders were overwhelmed in four days of vicious fighting. Again, only a handful of wounded prisoners was captured; the attackers had 700 casualties. The important islands of the Marshall group were now under American control.

Marines rest beside a captured Japanese pillbox on the Marshall Islands.

The Marianas

ADMIRAL NIMITZ decided to bypass the main Japanese Pacific stronghold of Truk. His Navy and Army aircraft were able to neutralize Truk — preventing the Japanese from using it effectively as either an air or naval base. But a direct amphibious attack against its formidable fortifications would have caused terrible loss of life among the American attackers. Nimitz decided, therefore, to "leapfrog" over Truk to the Marianas Islands.

These islands were more than one thousand miles west of Eniwetok, and only fifteen hundred miles south of the main islands of Japan. Nimitz' planners knew that the Marianas would be strongly defended, and that the Japanese would certainly do everything they could to destroy the American naval support forces and the troop convoys.

Overall responsibility for the invasion was given to Vice Admiral Raymond A. Spruance, who commanded the powerful Fifth Fleet. As before, the amphibious force was commanded by Admiral Turner. Under him, the assault force was again commanded by newly promoted Lieutenant General H. M. Smith. This force of three and a half Marine divisions and two Army divisions was divided between Smith's V Marine Amphibious Corps and the III Amphibious Corps under Major General Roy S. Geiger.

As the invasion convoys headed westward from Hawaii and the Marshalls, Admiral Spruance's carrier planes mercilessly hammered Japanese positions in the Marianas. On June 13, surface vessels began to join the terrific bombardment of Saipan. Two days later, on June 15, the 2nd and 4th Marine divisions of the V Corps landed on the south shores of Saipan. Next day the Army 27th Division also went ashore. As had been expected, they met the most determined resistance yet encountered in the Central Pacific fighting.

The first wave of Marines hits the Saipan beach in the Marianas, June, 1944.

While the Battle of Saipan was raging, Admiral Geiger's III Corps was approaching Guam, where it was scheduled to land on June 18. Suddenly, Admiral Spruance ordered the convoy to turn eastward, away from the Marianas. Patrol planes had sighted the Japanese fleet steaming eastward through the Philippine Sea. Spruance felt that it would be a mistake to make the landing in the middle of a great naval battle.

The Battle of the Philippine Sea lasted from June 19 to 21. Almost

Guam, July 1944. Marines take cover from Japanese fire after hitting the beach.

all of the action was at long range, by carrier strikes from the American and Japanese fleets. Spruance won a decisive victory, destroying most of the Japanese carrier planes and sinking many of the enemy ships. The Japanese had failed in their effort to interfere with the landings in the Marianas.

Meanwhile, extremely hard fighting continued in Saipan. During the height of the battle an argument broke out between Marine Corps General H. M. Smith, and Army Major General Ralph C. Smith, who commanded the 27th Division. The Marine commander complained that the Army division was not moving fast enough and not taking as many casualties as his Marine divisions. He did not think the 27th Division soldiers were fighting hard enough, and so he relieved Army General Smith from his command.

This clash between the two generals caused much controversy at the time, and the argument has continued since the war. Most military experts agree, however, that the effectiveness of a fighting force should not be measured in the number of casualties it suffers, but rather in the results it accomplishes.

Saipan was finally captured on July 9. The Japanese lost 27,000 killed and 2,000 captured. American casualties were about 3,500 killed and 13,000 wounded.

Because of the delay caused by the Battle of the Philippine Sea, General Geiger's preparations for the invasion of Guam had to be completely redone; the landings were postponed a month. On July 21 the Army's 77th Infantry Division, the 3rd Marine Division, and a Marine brigade assaulted Guam. Japanese resistance was almost as strong as on Saipan. But the island was finally captured by August 10. Meanwhile Marine units landed on Tinian on July 24 and captured it after nine days of intense combat. The principal islands of the Marianas were now firmly under American control.

The New Guinea Campaigns of 1944

The Admiralties

DURING the early weeks of 1944 Admiral Halsey's mixed Army-Navy-Marine force strengthened the bases seized in the Solomons. The most advanced of these, on Green Island, was less than one hundred air miles east of Rabaul. At the same time, the American and Australian troops of Krueger's Sixth Army cleared the southwestern portion of New Britain and also began to push northwest along the New Guinea coast.

The next important step in General MacArthur's plans was a proposed landing in the Admiralty Islands, lying west of New Britain. The Admiralties were important because of their airfields and harbors, and because the capture of these bases would complete the American ring around Rabaul. The invasion was scheduled for April, 1944.

In late February, General MacArthur decided that a bold attack on the Admiralties might catch the enemy by surprise, and also advance the Allied timetable by two months. MacArthur's staff was dismayed. They did not think such an attack could be successful without more troops and longer preparations. Despite almost unanimous advice against such a daring operation, MacArthur nonetheless ordered one division to make a "reconnaissance in force" — or exploratory probe — of Los Negros Island. Because his staff considered this operation so dangerous, MacArthur announced that he would personally accompany the leading unit ashore. He would then decide whether the attack should be continued, or whether to withdraw and wait to carry out the invasion in April.

As MacArthur had expected, the surprise assault was successful. His troops seized the vital airfield on Los Negros Island before the enemy realized what was happening. MacArthur, standing on the beach with the division commander decided that the attack should continue. "Hold what you have taken," he said, "no matter what the odds. Don't let go!"

Returning to his headquarters, MacArthur rushed reinforcements to Los Negros. The Japanese counterattacked violently, but the American troops repulsed them and forged ahead. By April, the entire Admiralty group was securely in American hands.

The Hollandia Campaign

DURING MARCH and early April, Australian troops on New Guinea pushed steadily westward from Saidor. They captured Madang on April 25. At this point, however, the reinforced Japanese Eighteenth Army stopped all Allied advance.

The Japanese high command had decided to make an all-out effort to hold western New Guinea. They had established a large supply and maintenance base at Hollandia, about five hundred miles west of Saidor, and beyond reach of MacArthur's fighter aircraft. Here they began to construct several airfields for future offensive and defensive air operations. By April, three of these were ready, located several miles inland behind the protection of coastal mountains.

The Japanese knew that General MacArthur had been very careful never to make an attack beyond the range of his land-based fighter aircraft — about 350 miles. Therefore, they had only a few security troops holding the Hollandia base. Most of the Eighteenth Army — now 65,000 strong — was concentrated between Madang and Wewak, where they expected MacArthur's next blow. The Jap-

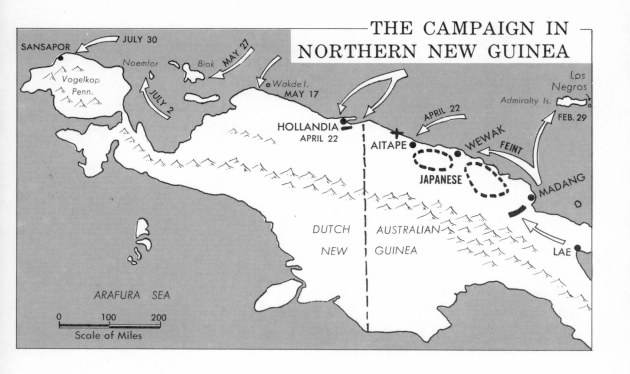

SANSAPOR JULY 30

Noemfor Biak MAY 27

Vogelkop Penn.

JULY 2

Wakde I. MAY 17

Los Negros

Admiralty Is. FEB. 29

HOLLANDIA APRIL 22

APRIL 22

AITAPE

WEWAK FEINT

JAPANESE

MADANG

DUTCH

NEW

AUSTRALIAN

GUINEA

LAE

ARAFURA SEA

0   100   200
Scale of Miles

anese were confident that they could repulse any new Australian-American attack.

General MacArthur outguessed the Japanese by deciding to make a five hundred-mile jump along the New Guinea coast to seize Hollandia itself. With the approval of the Joint Chiefs of Staff, Admiral Nimitz sent his Fast Carrier Task Force to help MacArthur with the air support and air cover necessary to the success of any large-scale amphibious operation. The Navy considered it very dangerous, however, to operate these carriers near the numerous uncaptured Jap-

Armed with war clubs, spears, and bows and arrows, natives of New Guinea spend a day or two marching up and down a newly-built Allied airstrip to pack the surface hard for aircraft landings.

anese air bases in New Guinea and the Caroline Islands. For this reason Admiral Nimitz insisted that the carriers could remain in the coastal waters of New Guinea for only four days.

MacArthur knew that it would invite disaster to leave the beaches and the troop convoys open to air attack after the carriers had left the area. This might permit the Japanese to isolate the assault forces, and then to overwhelm them in counterattacks. It was therefore essential to the success of the assault on Hollandia to obtain a secure base for land-based fighters before the carriers withdrew. MacArthur could not be sure that his attacking troops could seize the three inland airfields near Hollandia quickly enough. And he knew that any earlier attempt to seize other airfields in range of Hollandia would alert the Japanese, who would then rush reinforcements to protect their valuable base.

MacArthur solved this problem by planning to have two American regiments land at Aitape, about 125 miles east of Hollandia, at the same time that the Navy carriers were supporting the main landing of two divisions near Hollandia. Aitape was west of the main concentration of the Japanese Eighteenth Army, yet it was within extreme range of American airfields 350 miles to the east. The Aitape assault, therefore, could be covered by land-based aircraft from these bases while the carriers were assisting the main landing. MacArthur and his engineers were sure that the Aitape airfield could be made ready for use before the carriers had to withdraw. Then land-based air

U.S. tanks thread their way up Pancake Hill during the invasion of White Beach, Hollandia, New Guinea.

U.S. Infantry troops landing on Hollandia beach.

cover from Aitape would replace carrier air support at Hollandia.

The plan worked perfectly. In mid-April, to prevent the Japanese from interfering at either Hollandia or Aitape, Australian troops increased their pressure on the main Japanese army near Madang. This caused the Japanese to weaken their garrison at Hollandia still further by transferring troops to Wewak.

On April 22, the American 24th and 41st divisions landed on beaches 25 miles apart, west and east of Hollandia. With excellent carrier air support they converged inland against the Japanese airfields. In five days they had seized the entire Hollandia region, losing less than 100 men killed and about 1,000 wounded. The Japanese left about 5,000 dead behind them, while the survivors dispersed into the jungle.

The landing of two regiments at Aitape was equally successful; the airstrip was ready by April 24, two days ahead of schedule. Japanese resistance, however, was stiffer than at Hollandia. The Americans lost 450 killed and 2,500 wounded. More than 9,000 Japanese were killed.

The remainder of the Japanese Eighteenth Army, some fifty thousand strong, was now left isolated between Madang and Wewak. Without roads for overland movements, with no air or naval support, the Japanese were helpless. All their efforts to move forces over the narrow jungle trails were smashed by watchful Allied aircraft.

The Hollandia operation was one of the most brilliant actions of World War II. An entire Japanese army was encircled, and its effectiveness completely destroyed. Yet because of excellent planning and skillful coordination of land, sea, and air forces, the actual combat actions were relatively small, and only minor enemy forces were en-

New Guinea natives drag away a 13th Air Force C-47 after it crash landed in the nearby hills. Mistreated by the Japanese, they would do almost anything for the white man. They saved literally thousands of downed fliers.

gaged and defeated. This was typical of the tactics and strategy of General MacArthur's campaigns.

Conclusion of Operations in New Guinea

WITHOUT pause or hesitation, MacArthur's troops continued their leapfrog advance westward along the New Guinea coast. On May 17, they seized Wakde Island. Ten days later, a division landed on the powerful Japanese fortress of Biak Island. They encountered fanatical resistance, and captured the island only after a month of bitter fighting. While Biak was still being secured, another landing was made on July 2 on neighboring Noemfoor Island. On July 30, Allied troops made their final amphibious operation in New Guinea by landing at Sansapor, on the Vogelkop Peninsula — the northwestern tip of New Guinea — against little opposition.

By the end of July, 1944, General MacArthur had effectively conquered the entire northern coast of New Guinea, although more than 100,000 Japanese troops were still scattered in isolated areas for a distance of over 1,000 miles along that coast. About 100,000 helpless Japanese troops were also cut off around Rabaul on New Britain, and scattered through the Solomon Islands.

In the New Guinea campaign, General MacArthur's troops killed 35,000 Japanese. Their own losses had been less than 2,500 killed and about 16,000 wounded. In all of military history there is no instance of comparable results in territory gained and losses inflicted, at such a small cost in life. This was due to the way in which MacArthur had bypassed the main centers of Japanese resistance, defeating them by encirclement and envelopment, with excellent naval and air support.

69

The Return to the Philippines

The Preliminaries

DURING the summer of 1944, there was an intense debate in the Joint Chiefs of Staff about future strategy against Japan. Now that Mac-Arthur's troops had seized the ·coast of New Guinea, and Nimitz' forces were completing the conquest of the Marianas, Navy leaders urged that the Americans should bypass the powerful Japanese defenses of the Philippines. They wanted to seize bases in Formosa and on the east coast of China from which to make a final attack upon Japan. This meant that the main American effort against Japan would be made by Admiral Nimitz' Central Pacific Command, and that most of General MacArthur's troops would be sent to Nimitz to carry out the final campaigns.

The Army Chief of Staff, General George C. Marshall, however, believed that the next logical step would be for General MacArthur to advance from New Guinea to the Philippines, which would then become the base for a joint Army-Navy assault on Japan. He and his staff saw no need to become involved in lengthy operations either on Formosa or in China.

At a conference at Pearl Harbor in late July, President Roosevelt decided in favor of the Army plan. General MacArthur attended the conference, and his personal eloquence and logical presentation persuaded Roosevelt that attacks against Formosa and China would be far more costly of American lives. MacArthur also pointed out that the United States had a moral obligation to liberate the loyal people of the Philippine Islands as soon as possible.

Following this debate, there was close cooperation between Ad-

American civilians surrounded by Japanese soldiers in the Philippines.

miral Nimitz and General MacArthur in preparing for the advance to the Philippines. They planned a landing on Mindanao in November, to be followed by an attack on Leyte in late December. In preparation for these operations, MacArthur's Army and Navy forces landed on Morotai, in the Halmahera Islands, on September 15. That same day, Navy and Army forces of Nimitz' command assaulted the Palaus.

Admiral Halsey's Third Fleet, covering these preliminary operations, had been striking powerful carrier blows at Yap, Mindanao, and the central Philippines. Japanese resistance was so weak that Halsey concluded that the Japanese could no longer prevent an attack against the central Philippines. He radioed Admiral Nimitz, recommending an early move against Leyte, without bothering with Mindanao.

Nimitz knew that it usually takes at least two months to plan and prepare for an amphibious operation. But he had an amphibious force already loading to carry out an attack on Yap. He offered to turn this force over to General MacArthur's command for the landing which Halsey recommended.

MacArthur's staff rapidly calculated the problems of preparing for a large amphibious operation. Within twenty-four hours MacArthur informed Nimitz and the Joint Chiefs of Staff that he would be ready to attack Leyte on October 20 instead of December 20. This gave him, his staff, and his troops only thirty-five days to make plans, to load the necessary supplies, to move the troops to seaports, to put them on board ship, and to sail from their bases to Leyte.

"I Have Returned."

ON OCTOBER 19 two tremendous amphibious assault forces approached the east coast of Leyte. Admiral Theodore S. Wilkinson's Third Amphibious Force brought the X Corps from Hawaii as promised by Admiral Nimitz. The Seventh Amphibious Assault Force, under Admiral Daniel E. Barbey, brought MacArthur's XXIV Corps from the Southwest Pacific. Together these comprised the Sixth Army, commanded by General Krueger, under MacArthur. Totaling almost 100,000 combat troops, they were loaded on 350 transports and cargo ships, plus 400 other smaller amphibious craft.

Admiral Thomas C. Kinkaid's Seventh Fleet was assigned to cover the landing. This fleet included six of the old battleships that had been put out of action by the Japanese at Pearl Harbor. It also in-

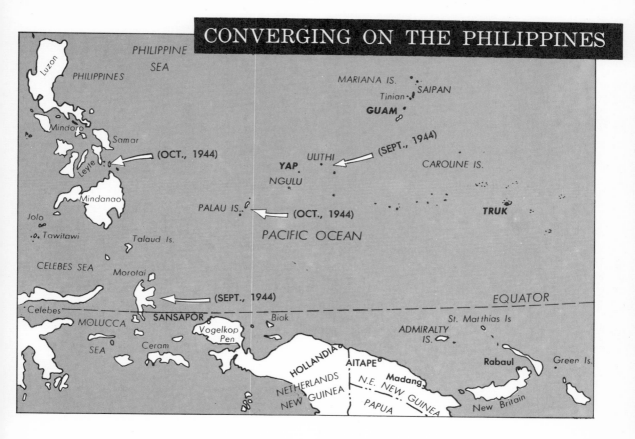

cluded eighteen escort carriers, whose planes had already begun a furious pre-assault bombardment. These carriers would provide air cover and air support to the troops once they were ashore.

Further out to sea lay Admiral Halsey's mighty Third Fleet, the most powerful naval force ever assembled. Halsey's planes had joined with Kinkaid's in pounding the beaches at Leyte and in sweep-

73

ing up and down the northern and southern Philippines to hammer at all Japanese bases, and to prevent any Japanese naval opposition to the landing.

At 10:00 A.M. on October 20, 1944, under the cover of a terrific naval gunfire bombardment, the assault waves of the X and XXIV Corps swept toward the beaches on a front eighteen miles long. While the leading elements were still fighting to secure the beaches, General MacArthur, accompanied by President Sergio Osmena of the Philippine Commonwealth (former President Quezon had died), splashed ashore from an assault landing craft. Speaking into the microphone of a portable radio transmitter, MacArthur broadcast a message to the 17 million loyal people of the Philippines, who had been waiting for him for two and a half years:

"I have returned. By the grace of Almighty God our forces stand again on Philippine soil. Rally to me! Rise and strike!"

WIDE WORLD PHOTOS

General Douglas MacArthur (left) with his chief of staff, Lieutenant N. Richard Sutherland, wades through the surf as he returns to the Philippines to direct the invasion. October 10, 1944.

The Battle of Leyte

EVEN BEFORE the American landings, the Japanese had been preparing for a major naval counterblow. All of the remaining combat elements of the Japanese fleet, from bases in Japan, in Borneo, and in Singapore, converged toward the Philippines. Their plan was to lure Admiral Halsey's Third Fleet away from the landing area, and then to strike with their main force against Admiral Kinkaid's Seventh Fleet and against General MacArthur's transports. They hoped to be able to defeat Kinkaid and to destroy the entire transport convoy, thus permitting Japanese land troops to overwhelm the American troops already ashore.

The Japanese plan was a good one, and it came close to working. It brought on the greatest naval battle in the history of the world. It also gave a terrific scare to all of the American Army and Navy commanders. But the final result of the battle for Leyte Gulf was a tremendous American victory, and the effective elimination of the Japanese navy as an obstacle to further American operations in the Western Pacific.

While this gigantic naval struggle was taking place between October 23 and 26, General Krueger's Sixth Army was establishing itself firmly ashore. But the American soldiers were encountering the fiercest kind of opposition.

Field Marshal Count Terauchi, overall Japanese commander in Southeast Asia and the Philippines, issued orders that Leyte must be held at all costs. He ordered General Tomoyuki Yamashita, conqueror of Malaya and Singapore, to take direct charge of the Sixteenth Army defending Leyte. Terauchi and Yamashita had 260,000 troops in the Philippines, and they knew that mountainous Leyte was easily defendable. They rushed reinforcements to the island by trans-

75

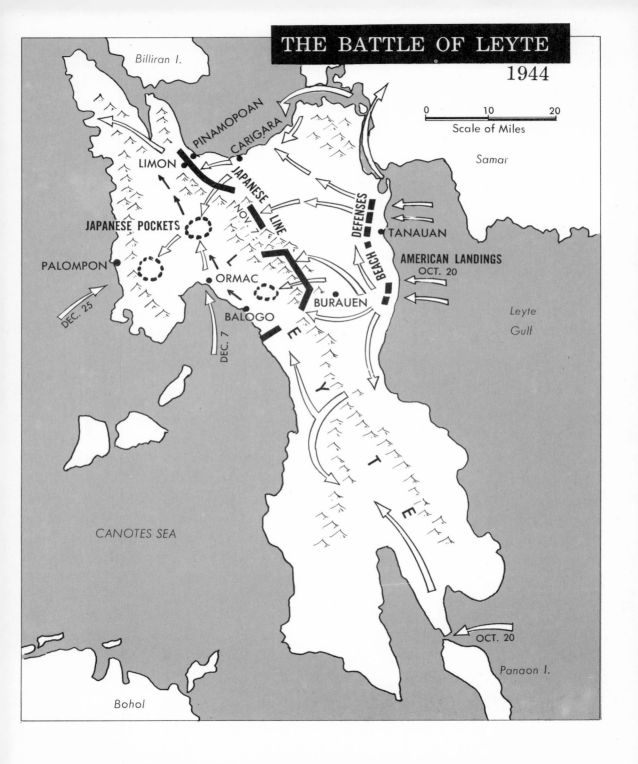

THE BATTLE OF LEYTE
1944

Billiran I.

PINAMOPOAN

CARIGARA

LIMON

JAPANESE LINE

NOV.

JAPANESE POCKETS

PALOMPON

ORMAC

BALOGO

DEC. 7

DEC. 25

DEFENSES

TANAUAN

BEACH

AMERICAN LANDINGS
OCT. 20

BURAUEN

Samar

Scale of Miles

0   10   20

Leyte
Gulf

L E Y T E

CANOTES SEA

OCT. 20

Panaon I.

Bohol

Army troops watch for sniper fire shortly after coming ashore on Leyte.

ports and naval escort vessels. Japanese army and navy planes violently attacked the American carriers in an effort to gain control of the air over the beaches. Here, for the first time, the Japanese used *Kamikaze* (suicide plane) tactics.

The aerial struggle was the most intense of the Pacific war, but Navy planes, assisted by Army Air Force fighters on hastily created landing strips near the beaches, finally gained control of the air. Below them the soldiers forged ahead. During the first two weeks of the campaign they seized most of Leyte's northeastern coastal plain.

Living quarters of Marine night fighter pilots on Leyte in the Philippines.

The battle now became a slugging match between veteran attackers and veteran defenders in the rugged, difficult mountains of central Leyte. Yamashita rushed reinforcements to Leyte by convoys from Luzon and other islands.

During November and early December, American Army and Navy fighter planes reduced, and then completely stopped, the Japanese reinforcement convoys. Losses in transports and small naval vessels became so heavy that the Japanese could not risk any more. Only a small trickle of Japanese reinforcements continued to reach Leyte, moving by sailboat at night.

General Krueger now began a double envelopment of the remaining Japanese forces in central Leyte. On the right, Major General Franklin C. Sibert's X Corps swung southwest to try to smash its way through the Japanese stronghold of Limon, while Major General John R. Hodge's XXIV Corps struck northwestward toward Ormoc. On December 7 the 77th Division made an amphibious landing five miles east of Ormoc.

Violent rainstorms and deep mud interfered with the supply lines of both the Americans and Japanese. The roads were impassable for American motor vehicles, and so supplies had to be carried to the front by hand. Casualties were brought to the rear by Filipino bearers.

Finally the pressure was too much for the Japanese. On December 21 the exhausted remnants of their veteran 1st Division broke and fled from their last-stand positions near Ormoc. Although fighting would continue in the mountains of western Leyte for several weeks, for all practical purposes the Battle of Leyte was over.

Back to Lingayen

GENERAL MACARTHUR's next objective was the island of Luzon. Krueger's Sixth Army again provided the assault force. In December in a preliminary landing in Mindoro, it seized advanced air bases. During the first week of January Krueger's force sailed from Leyte Gulf under a strong naval escort, through the narrow straits of the central Philippine Islands, and into the South China Sea. Air cover was provided by escort carriers, and by planes from Mindoro.

Further cover for this bold advance through waters and islands still controlled by Japanese forces was provided by American Army and Navy planes attacking targets all through the Philippines. Their objective was not only to divert Japanese attention from Krueger's movement, but also to destroy roads, bridges, and tunnels which General Yamashita might use to shift troops to meet the new assault. American and Filipino guerrilla forces in southern Luzon also increased their activity to attract Japanese attention. American minesweepers and other ships approached several beaches on the coast of Luzon, and elsewhere in the Philippines, to make the Japanese think that landings were intended at some of these many points.

But Krueger's objective was Lingayen Gulf, where Homma and his army had landed three years and one month earlier. This time Krueger's army consisted of the I and XIV Corps. They hit the beaches at the head of Lingayen Gulf on the morning of January 9, 1945. By night 68,000 troops had been landed, and controlled a beachhead 15 miles long and 6,000 yards deep.

Although the Japanese knew that Lingayen Gulf was the best place for a landing on Luzon, they had never expected that the Americans would move so boldly and so far from their original landing point on Leyte. This swift move — assisted by deception, air support, and guerrilla activity threw the Japanese into confusion.

Luzon Campaign

THE SIXTH ARMY's advance toward Manila was rapid. To prevent the Japanese from following his example of retreating into the fastnesses of Bataan, on January 29 General MacArthur sent two divisions of the XI Corps ashore northwest of that peninsula. They drove quickly eastward to make contact with the main forces of the Sixth Army moving southward from Lingayen. On January 30 a small force of American Rangers and Filipino guerrillas made a daring raid behind the Japanese lines to rescue several hundred Allied war prisoners at Cabanatuan.

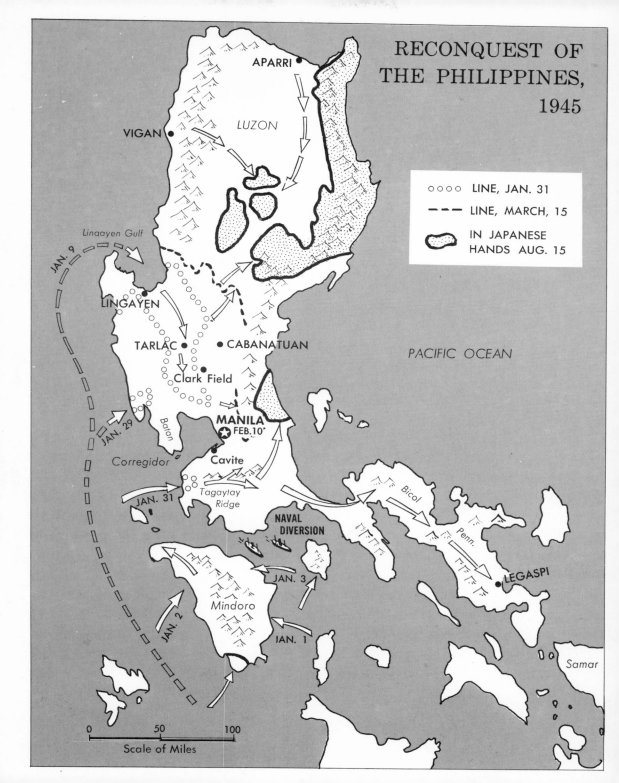

RECONQUEST OF THE PHILIPPINES, 1945

APARRI

LUZON

VIGAN

Legend:
- ○○○○ LINE, JAN. 31
- – – – LINE, MARCH, 15
- IN JAPANESE HANDS AUG. 15

Lingayen Gulf

JAN. 9

LINGAYEN

PACIFIC OCEAN

TARLAC ● CABANATUAN

Clark Field

JAN. 29

Bataan

MANILA
FEB. 10

Corregidor

Cavite

JAN. 31

Tagaytay Ridge

Bicol

NAVAL DIVERSION

JAN. 3

Penn.

JAN. 2

Mindoro

JAN. 1

LEGASPI

Samar

0   50   100
Scale of Miles

Next day part of the 11th Airborne Division of General Eichelberger's Eighth Army made an unopposed amphibious landing at Nasugbu, southwest of Manila. On February 2 the remainder of that division made a parachute drop on Tagaytay Ridge, and then began to head northward toward the naval base of Cavite. That same day troops of the 1st Cavalry Division of the Sixth Army reached the northeastern outskirts of Manila.

Advance troops take cover from Japanse fire on Luzon.

American forces then cleared the entire area around Manila Bay, including Bataan Peninsula. Meanwhile, other troops closed in on the Japanese still holding Manila. Though their position was hopeless, the garrison in the city fought bitterly from house to house. It was not until February 23 that organized resistance ended.

On February 16, while the fight was still raging in the battered city, a combined American airborne and amphibious assault struck Corregidor. For two weeks the Japanese struggled bitterly to hold the island. The battle ended only when the defenders, surrounded in tunnels that the Americans had built before the war, blew themselves up. Later, a total of 4,215 dead Japanese were counted; nobody knows how many died in the tunnels. Of the 3,000 Americans who took part in the Battle of Corregidor, 140 were killed and 530 wounded.

By the beginning of March, Manila Bay was open to Allied vessels. In less than two months General MacArthur had accomplished what the Japanese had taken six months to do. The American and Japanese situations had been quite similar. In 1945, General Yamashita, like General MacArthur in 1941-42, was cut off from his home supply. He was opposed — on the same battlefields — by an enemy who had overwhelming air superiority. Neither the Japanese nor the American general could expect any assistance from any other area.

There were, however, some differences. In the first Luzon Campaign, MacArthur had a partly trained army, with only a few regular troops. Moreover, he was short of supplies and equipment. In 1945, Yamashita had over 235,000 first-line Japanese troops on Luzon, and he had had two years to prepare after the Americans had begun their offensives at Guadalcanal and Buna. On the other hand, on both occasions General MacArthur had the good will of the Filipino people, and, in his final operations against Yamashita, the assistance of the

A Japanese water tank trap, left by the retreating Japanese, fails to retard the onslaught of the American invasion.

effective guerrilla forces which he had created. Superior military genius and ingenuity had brought decisive victory. There could be no clearer proof of this than in the ratio of lives lost: twenty-four Japanese dead to every American killed.

In February and March, Eighth Army troops landed in other areas of the Philippines, rapidly extending American control over most of the islands. As usual, the principal Japanese fortifications were avoided. During April and May the Sixth Army extended its hold on Luzon, while the Eighth spread over most of Mindanao. Japanese resistance followed its usual stubborn, fanatical pattern, but by June the Japanese troops had been driven into the inaccessible jungle regions of the high Philippine mountains. Here they remained, unable to interfere with the Allied consolidation, until Japan surrendered.

On May 1, an amphibious force of Australian and Netherlands East Indies troops landed on Tarakan Island off the northeast coast of Borneo. By the end of the month, all important installations on this oil-rich island were in Allied hands. In June, the Australians also seized Brunei Bay, in northwest Borneo, which gave the Allies possession of important naval anchorages, airfields, and more oil fields. On July 1, the Australians seized Balikpapan, in southeastern Borneo. The Southern Resources Area was again changing hands.

The U.S. Eighth Army on Mindanao Island.

The Battle of Iwo Jima

Importance of Iwo

DURING the summer and early fall of 1944, American engineers were busy building tremendous airfields and supply installations on the Marianas Islands of Saipan, Guam, and Tinian. As the construction work approached completion, vast quantities of supplies, gasoline, and bombs began to arrive in Navy cargo ships. Then squadrons of new B-29 Superfortress bombers began to fly into the fields.

On November 24, 1944, the B-29 squadrons made their first attack on Tokyo. This was a round-trip flight of three thousand miles; most of the load carried by the great planes was gasoline, so that they could not carry many bombs. Nevertheless, they did considerable damage. In the following weeks, the long-range raids from the Marianas continued to strike Japan in ever-increasing numbers and intensity.

Japanese reaction was fierce. Antiaircraft guns and fighter planes concentrated against the Superfortresses. Many damaged planes and their crews went down in the ocean as they tried to make the long trip back to the Marianas.

Almost midway between Tokyo and the Marianas bases lay the rocky, heavily fortified island of Iwo Jima. This was the only island in the Bonin and Volcano island groups suitable for airfields. The Japanese rushed fighter planes to the one small airfield already there, and immediately began construction of two more airfields. In addition, Japanese bombers from Iwo made a number of damaging raids against the Marianas.

American bombers, carrier planes, and surface ships struck back at Iwo Jima. In late 1944, the American Joint Chiefs of Staff ordered Admiral Nimitz to seize the island. This would eliminate Japanese attacks against the B-29's and against their bases. Furthermore, the island would be extremely useful in American hands. Fighters could be based on Iwo to escort the Superfortresses in their attacks against the Japanese mainland. Also, crippled B-29's returning from Japan could make emergency landings on the island's airfields.

Iwo Jima is only eight square miles of waterless volcanic rock and sand. It is honeycombed with caves and interconnecting tunnels. In

U.S. Army infantrymen and a Marine on Iwo Jima advance on a cave where they suspect Japanese soldiers are hidden.

1944, these led to well-concealed and strongly protected Japanese pillboxes and covered gun positions scattered throughout the island. The underground shelters had many exits, and all of these were carefully concealed by camouflage. Every square yard of the island and of the water approaches to it could be covered by an intensive fire from many Japanese guns and heavy mortars. Minefields had been laid not only on the beaches but also completely across the island.

General Tadamichi Kuribayashi and his 21,000 troops had each taken a solemn oath to defend the island to the last man, and "to kill ten of the enemy before dying." Iwo Jima was probably the strongest single fortification assaulted by any troops during World War II.

The Assault

BEGINNING in December, and continuing through January and most of February, the Americans attacked Iwo Jima every day by land-based bombers from the Marianas, or by carrier planes, or both. In addition, American naval forces frequently hammered it with long-range gunfire.

On February 16, 1945, the intensity of the air attacks increased; a naval task force of six battleships and numerous cruisers and destroyers began a pre-assault bombardment. By dawn of February 19, Iwo Jima had sustained the most intensive bombardment ever placed on a target of that size.

As in all of the other important Central Pacific assaults, the commander of the amphibious task force was Vice Admiral Turner, while the assault force commander was Marine Lieutenant General H. M. Smith. The V Marine Amphibious Corps, 75,000 men strong, comprising the 3rd, 4th and 5th Divisions, swept ashore on the south-

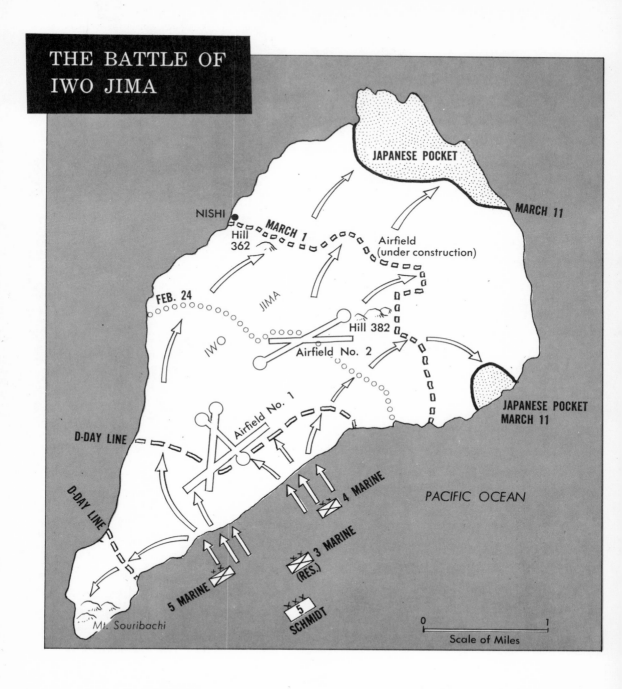

THE BATTLE OF IWO JIMA

JAPANESE POCKET

NISHI

MARCH 1

Hill 362

Airfield (under construction)

MARCH 11

FEB. 24

IWO   JIMA

Hill 382

Airfield No. 2

JAPANESE POCKET
MARCH 11

D-DAY LINE

Airfield No. 1

D-DAY LINE

PACIFIC OCEAN

4 MARINE

3 MARINE
(RES.)

5 MARINE

5
SCHMIDT

Mt. Souribachi

0   1
Scale of Miles

U.S. Marines are pinned down briefly by enemy fire as they hit the beach at Iwo Jima, February 19, 1945.

eastern beaches of the island at 9:00 A.M. on February 19. The first waves of the Marines discovered that the tremendous bombardment had blown up many of the mines along the beaches, and had also destroyed other obstacles which the Japanese had laid along the water's edge. But they also soon learned that the bombardment had broken neither the fighting spirit nor the fighting capabilities of the defenders.

During the bombardment the Japanese had taken refuge in their deep, underground shelters, while a few lookouts, in strongly protected concrete observation posts, watched for the arrival of the attackers. As the pre-assault fire lifted from the areas near the beaches, the Japanese jumped out of their shelters. They at once laid heavy fire against the Marines arriving on the beaches, and against the waves of landing craft still approaching from the transports offshore.

Marine privates use flame throwers against the mighty defenses that block the way to Iwo Jima's Mount Suribachi.

DEFENSE DEPARTMENT PHOTO (MARINE CORPS)

The Fifth Marine Division lands near Mount Suribachi on Iwo Jima.

The Marines began to suffer heavy casualties, and for a while the advance was held up. Gunfire from the supporting warships searched for the Japanese gun positions and silenced a few. But the defenders kept raining destruction on the beaches.

Nevertheless, waves of landing craft with reinforcements continued to arrive. Despite their casualties, and despite the fearful danger, the Marines began to move forward. By nightfall they had driven all the way across the southwestern portion of the island. The defenders of strongly fortified Mount Suribachi, on the southwestern tip of Iwo, were isolated.

92

For four days a vicious hand-to-hand battle raged around Mount Suribachi before the position was finally taken on February 23. Though still under heavy fire from the main Japanese positions, a group of Marines raised an American flag on the summit of the hill.

The small flag, actually the first to fly over Iwo Jima, is replaced by the larger flag featured in the famous photograph.

During these days high winds and heavy seas interfered greatly with sending supplies and reinforcements ashore. The ammunition supply of the troops ashore fell perilously low. This meant that the gunfire-support ships had to increase their rate of fire, and they also began to run out of ammunition.

On February 25, however, the weather cleared, permitting more ammunition and supplies to be rushed to the beaches. In the calmer weather, also, supply ships brought more naval ammunition to the gunfire-support vessels. The crisis of the Battle of Iwo Jima was over, though three weeks more of desperate fighting lay ahead.

Inch by inch, yard by yard, gun position by gun position, the Marines fought their way north and east across the island. Finally, on March 17, General Smith was able to announce officially that organized resistance had been overcome. Individual Japanese, still taking refuge in hidden caves, nevertheless continued to fight for many days more.

The Results

Over 21,000 Japanese were killed on Iwo Jima, and more than 200 were taken prisoner. But the exact number of Japanese dead will never be known, since many were sealed up in their underground shelters.

The battle had been a costly one for the Americans, who suffered almost 25,000 casualties, nearly 7,000 being killed. Yet, though these losses were heavy, it is surprising that they were not worse, since the small size of the island made maneuver impossible, and the Marines had no choice but to attack frontally against the most formidable defenses they encountered during the war.

Wounded Marines on Iwo Jima are helped to an aid station by medical corpsmen.

In a way that is rarely proven so clearly, the American losses were justified by the results. Before the end of the war more than 2,250 B-29's, carrying about 25,000 crewmen, made emergency landings on the airfields of Iwo Jima. Most of these planes and men would probably have been lost if the Marines had not sacrificed themselves to capture the island.

Okinawa Campaign

American Plans and Forces

LATE IN 1944, the Joint Chiefs of Staff ordered Admiral Nimitz to invade the Ryukyu Islands as soon as possible after the capture of Iwo Jima. These islands would be used for air and naval bases to support landings on the main Japanese islands. The capture of the Ryukyus would also cut Japan's sea communications to her island and mainland territories further south.

Except for Okinawa, all of the islands in the Ryukyu group are small and rocky. Okinawa is sixty-five miles long, and varies in width from two to eighteen miles. It has much flat area, suitable for airfields, and its long, uneven coastline provides good naval anchorages. So Okinawa was chosen as the principal target for Admiral Nimitz' invasion effort.

The invasion of Okinawa had many other special problems which Nimitz' staff planners and combat troops had not previously experienced. This was the first time that American forces had been required to fight in a large area inhabited by a hostile, Japanese, local population.

The most difficult problems were those caused by Okinawa's distance from any large American supporting and supply bases. A tremendous invasion force would be necessary to capture such a large and well-defended island, therefore many supply ships would be required to make the long round trips from Okinawa to Hawaii or San Francisco. All of the initial air support would have to be supplied by naval carriers, and much bomber support would be required from the carriers throughout the operation, even after the capture of

96

fighter airfields ashore. Also, since Okinawa was within easy striking range of air bases in Japan, the Navy would have to provide protection against expected air attacks. These things contributed to make this the most difficult planning problem which any American staff had encountered so far during the war.

To carry out the invasion, Admiral Nimitz established a unified amphibious force, under Admiral Raymond Spruance, commanding the Fifth Fleet. The actual amphibious operations were to be directed, as before in the Central Pacific area, by Vice Admiral Turner. The expeditionary force was the Tenth Army, commanded by Lieutenant General Simon B. Buckner, Jr. His army consisted of five Army and three Marine divisions, numbering about 225,000 combat troops, plus an equal number of support and garrison troops.

After a careful study by Army, Navy, and Marine Corps staffs, it was decided that the best landing beaches were those on the west coast of Okinawa, near the town of Hagushi. These beaches were protected from the open sea. Also, there were two nearby airfields which, it was hoped, the assault troops could quickly overrun and capture.

Japanese Plans and Forces

THE JAPANESE realized that Okinawa was a likely target for an American invasion. The island was garrisoned by the Thirty-Second Army, totaling about 140,000 men, under Lieutenant General Mitsuru Ushijima. The natural defensive strength of Okinawa's mountains was increased by powerful fortifications, particularly in the southern part of the island.

With the Japanese high command in Tokyo, Ushijima worked out a plan which would make the maximum use of the dwindling naval and air resources of Japan. Most of her trained airplane pilots had been killed in the disastrous battles of 1943 and 1944. And most of Japan's combat vessels had been sunk.

But the Japanese navy and air force had many brave, untrained men who were willing to sacrifice their lives for their country. So the Japanese navy secretly moved 350 motor-torpedo boats to the Kerama Islands off the southwestern coast of Okinawa, and concealed them there. These boats, loaded with high explosives, were really large, manned torpedoes. The volunteer suicide crews were to ram and sink American warships and transports gathered for the landing near Hagushi Bay. At the same time a force of *Kamikaze* suicide airplane pilots were to fly their explosive-laden planes into other vessels of the American fleet.

Ushijima intended to permit the Americans to get ashore without opposition, so that he could do the greatest possible damage by combined land, sea, and air counteroffensive. His plan was to attack the troops who had come ashore while the suicide boats and planes were smashing the invasion fleet.

The Assault

AMERICAN preparations for the invasion began early in March, with long-range air strikes against Okinawa itself as well as against all Japanese air bases in southern Japan, in China, and on Formosa. These coordinated air operations were carried out by Admiral Nimitz' carrier task forces, by General MacArthur's air forces in the Philippines, and by the B-29's in the Marianas. During the last days of March, as the vast invasion armada of 1,200 ships approached the Ryukyus, the air assaults increased in intensity.

On March 26, the 77th Infantry Division made a sudden, surprise

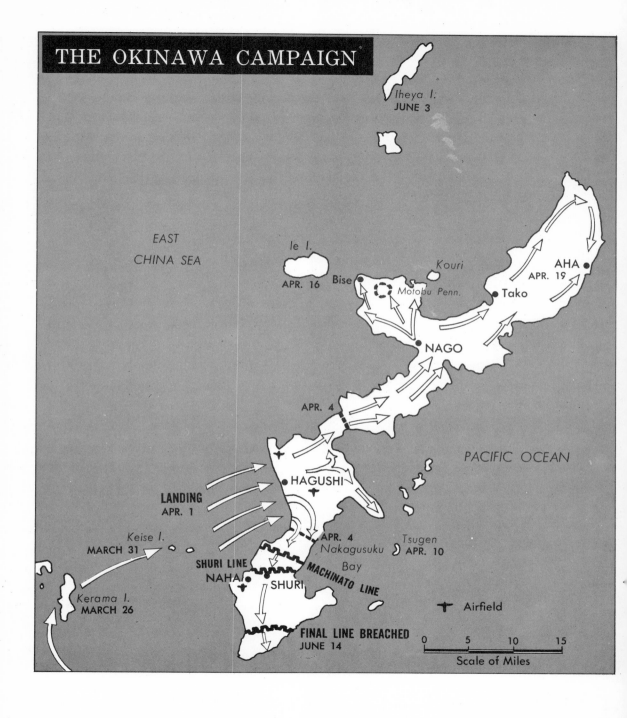

THE OKINAWA CAMPAIGN

Iheya I.
JUNE 3

EAST

CHINA SEA

Ie I.
APR. 16

Kouri

Bise

Motobu Penn.

AHA
APR. 19

Tako

NAGO

APR. 4

PACIFIC OCEAN

HAGUSHI

LANDING
APR. 1

Keise I.
MARCH 31

APR. 4

Tsugen
APR. 10

Nakagusuku

SHURI LINE

NAHA

Bay

MACHINATO LINE

SHURI

Kerama I.
MARCH 26

FINAL LINE BREACHED
JUNE 14

✛ Airfield

0   5   10   15

Scale of Miles

landing in the Kerama Islands. Five days later it captured the nearby Keise Islands. The Keramas would be used as an advanced naval anchorage, while long-range artillery would be placed on the Keises to cover the landings. The Japanese had not foreseen these moves. The seizure of the Kerama Islands resulted in the capture of all the suicide motor-torpedo boats they had hidden there. This ruined an important part of the Japanese defensive plan.

During the early hours of April 1, the great amphibious armada approached Okinawa. Hundreds of naval vessels, ranging in size from battleships to small rocket-support vessels, joined swarms of carrier bombers and fighters in placing on the Hagushi beaches the heaviest assault bombardments yet undertaken. Shortly after dawn, the 2nd Marine Division pretended to land at several places along the southeastern coast of the island, attracting Japanese attention there.

At 8:30 A.M., an eight-mile-long line of landing craft swept onto the Hagushi beaches. On the north were the 1st and 6th Marine divisions of the III Marine Amphibious Corps, under General Geiger. The right-hand part of the line was made up of units from the 7th and 96th Infantry divisions of General John R. Hodge's XXIV Army Corps.

As the troops poured ashore, they realized for the first time that the tremendous bombardment had fallen into an area where there were no defending troops. Unaware of General Ushijima's plan to let them get ashore before attacking them, the Americans could not understand why they met no opposition in the landing. They were grateful, however, and more than fifty thousand American troops, including supporting artillery, landed in the first eight hours of the invasion.

In the next few days, Ushijima's troops fell back toward the hills south of the landing. They offered little resistance, since they were

Marines fire at a group of eight Japanese changing positions.

preparing to counterattack in coordination with the planned *Kamikaze* suicide air strikes from Japan.

The Kamikazes

THE FIRST IMPORTANT *Kamikaze* attacks came on April 6, and caused much damage to American transports and warships. That same day, in an attempt to make up for the loss of the motor-torpedo boat flo-

A Japanese suicide plane misses the USS Sangamon and crashes alongside it.

tilla in the Keramas, a naval task force of ten vessels sped from Japan toward Okinawa to join in the attack. One of these was the giant battleship *Yamato*, largest warship in the world at the time. But on April 7, American carrier planes sank the *Yamato* and five other vessels; the four remaining escaped back to Japan, seriously damaged. There was no further Japanese naval interference with the invasion.

The *Kamikaze* attacks continued, however. But once they had learned the Japanese suicide tactics, the Americans were able to prevent the suicide planes from doing serious harm. Losses and damage continued, but the *Kamikazes* were never able to drive off the covering naval forces, as they had hoped.

Meanwhile, land operations were continuing. The Americans soon discovered that there were few Japanese troops in the northern part of the island. By mid-April they had cleared them all out. As a result, the 77th Division was able to seize nearby Ie Island, after a hard fight of five days. Work was immediately started to expand the airfield already existing on this island. When this field became operational, early in May, fighter planes based there took a heavy toll of the *Kamikazes* coming from Kyushu, in Japan.

Japanese "suicide plane" found on Yontan Airfield on Okinawa.

Battle for the Shuri Zone

MEANWHILE, in the southern portion of the island, the advance of the XXIV Corps was brought to an abrupt halt by Japanese counterattacks from the formidable Shuri Zone. This deep, interlocking complex of mountain forts extending across the island took advantage of broken ridges and steep cliffs. It was honeycombed with caves in which the Japanese sheltered themselves against American heavy artillery and air bombardment. Here Ushijima had concentrated 130,000 well-trained troops.

For three weeks the XXIV Corps hammered against the Shuri Zone. On April 24 they were finally able to force their way through a portion of the first line, but by April 28 all further forward advance had been completely stopped.

General Buckner now reorganized his forces for a renewed offensive. The conquest of the northern part of the island having been completed, he brought up the III Marine Corps and placed it on the right of the XXIV Corps. His plan was to have each of these corps make its main effort on the seaward flank, with the assistance of naval gunfire support. In this way he intended to envelope and encircle the main Japanese positions near Shuri.

On May 4, while the reorganization of Buckner's forces was under way, the Japanese made a major counterattack all along the line. Before dawn, under the cover of a mass *Kamikaze* air attack from Kyushu, they rushed out of their defenses. They were thrown back by converging American artillery and machine-gun fire and by ruthless strafing from fighter planes. Despite severe punishment, however, the Japanese continued the attacks in unreasoning fury for two days. Finally, after losses of more than five thousand men, Ushijima pulled his shattered troops back into their mountain strongholds. His best

U.S. Marines cover a Christian church whose steeple was used as a snipers' nest by the Japanese.

troops had been wasted, and he had disclosed hidden artillery positions which the American artillery and aircraft soon pounded into silence. The Americans had suffered one thousand casualties.

On May 11, the III and XXIV corps began Buckner's planned offensive. Systematically and deliberately they fought their way into and through the flanks of the Japanese positions. The advance was slow and costly, but the battlewise American troops could not be stopped by even the most fanatical Japanese resistance.

On May 21, Ushijima began a skillful withdrawal from the Shuri Zone to avoid the threatened encirclement. The Americans pressed after the retreating Japanese, but were unable to hurry or to confuse Ushijima's deliberate and skillful delaying actions.

The Conquest of Okinawa

DURING the early days of June, Ushijima organized a last-ditch defense in the mountainous southern tip of Okinawa. The Americans

Marines hurdle a stone wall as they drive across Okinawa.

DEFENSE DEPARTMENT PHOTO (MARINE CORPS)

began an assault of this rocky position on June 12. Again the III and the XXIV corps made converging and encircling drives around the center of the stronghold, smashing their way through and around Japanese pockets of resistance. The two spearheads met on June 20. All organized defense now collapsed, as Japanese troops, for the first time in the war, began surrendering in large numbers.

But General Buckner did not see this final victory he had planned. On June 18, two days before the end of the battle, he was at a Marine battalion forward observation post, peering at Japanese positions less than three hundred yards away. One of the few remaining Japanese artillery pieces scored a direct hit on the observation post, killing General Buckner immediately.

About 130,000 Japanese were killed in the campaign, and 7,400 prisoners were taken. American losses, including those on the warships providing naval and air cover, totaled over 13,000 killed and about 36,000 wounded. The Navy, in fact, suffered its heaviest losses of the entire war. Thirty-six vessels were sunk, and 368 warships, transports, and other vessels were damaged. Nearly 8,000 Japanese aircraft were destroyed; the Americans lost 763.

Now, with an outpost and a major base only 350 miles from Japan itself, the Americans were ready to start planning for their final invasion.

Final Victory

The Invasion Plans

During the summer of 1945, the tremendous armed might of the United States got ready to bring about the final destruction of the

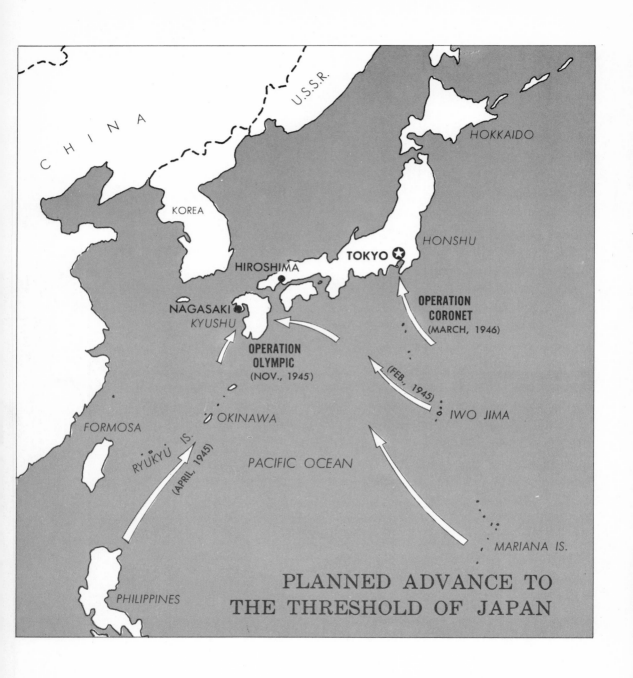

CHINA

U.S.S.R.

HOKKAIDO

KOREA

HIROSHIMA

HONSHU

TOKYO

NAGASAKI
KYUSHU

OPERATION
CORONET
(MARCH, 1946)

OPERATION
OLYMPIC
(NOV., 1945)

(FEB., 1945)

IWO JIMA

OKINAWA

FORMOSA

RYUKYU IS.

(APRIL, 1945)

PACIFIC OCEAN

MARIANA IS.

PHILIPPINES

PLANNED ADVANCE TO
THE THRESHOLD OF JAPAN

Japanese Empire. General MacArthur, Admiral Nimitz, and their staffs now began coordinated planning for invading Japan, while their forces paused briefly to prepare themselves for great amphibious assaults.

Landings were to be made on the island of Kyushu in November, and on Honshu in March. Troops from Germany were being brought

Twenty-four CM heavy artillery weapons at Nagasaki Kanamuna dump.

to the Pacific to take part in this last great battle. Meanwhile American long-range strategic bombers continued to hammer the Japanese mainland from their bases in the Marianas, spreading destruction, chaos, and confusion.

American planners knew that Japan was close to economic collapse as a result of the damage being done by American long-range air raids, and by the Navy blockade which cut Japan off from most of her overseas areas. They realized, therefore, that Japan *might* be willing to surrender, and to make peace before the American troops actually invaded.

But American military leaders could not be certain that Japan would surrender. In almost every battle, Japanese troops had fought to the very end, and most had preferred suicide to surrender. The United States could hardly believe that a nation would be willing to commit suicide rather than to make peace, but she could not be sure. Japan had at least two million well-trained, well-equipped ground troops on the four main islands. She had at least as many more in Manchuria and China.

Therefore, although they hoped that the Japanese would realize that further resistance was senseless and would only result in the loss of the lives of millions of soldiers and civilians, Allied leaders felt they had no choice but to continue their invasion plans. Meanwhile, in the Potsdam Declaration of early July, they promised Japan a just and honorable peace if she would surrender. They threatened the nation with complete destruction, however, if she continued the war.

The Surrender

IT WAS clear to the Japanese government that their nation had been defeated, but the idea of surrender was very distasteful to them.

While Japanese leaders were debating whether or not to accept the Potsdam Declaration, they tried to make contact with the Allies through the still-neutral Russian government. Russian dictator Stalin did not pass the message on, however. He was preparing to join in the war against Japan, in order to increase Soviet prestige and power in East Asia.

America now decided to prove to the Japanese that she was serious

Some of the 16-man Japanese delegation arrive at Ie Shima on the first leg of their journey to Manila to make surrender arrangements. Second from the left is the leader of the delegation, Lieutenant General Kawabe Takashiro, Vice Chief of the Imperial Staff. All the delegates carry the traditional samurai sword.

AIR FORCE PHOTO

in her threat of total destruction. The hope was that Japan could be shocked into making peace before both sides suffered terrible casualties in land battles within Japan itself. On August 6, 1945, therefore, an American B-29 dropped the first atomic bomb on the military base city of Hiroshima. About sixty thousand civilians and soldiers were killed by the bomb, more were injured, and over half of the city was wrecked. Three days later a second bomb dropped on Nagasaki, where Japanese losses were almost as great.

Fearful that the war would be ended before she got into it, Russia declared war against Japan on August 8, and Soviet troops began to invade Manchuria. On August 10, the Japanese government decided that it must make peace at once, and sent a message through Switzerland offering to surrender on the basis of the terms of the Potsdam Proclamation. The Allied governments accepted this surrender offer, and on August 14 (August 15 in the Far East) the fighting stopped.

On September 2, 1945, General MacArthur, as Supreme Commander for the Allied Powers, accepted the formal surrender of the Japanese nation on the deck of the United States battleship *Missouri* in Tokyo Bay. After nearly four years, the Pacific war with Japan was ended.

General of the Army Douglas MacArthur signs the surrender document at formal ceremonies aboard the USS Missouri in Tokyo Bay. Behind him are U.S. General Jonathan Wainwright (left) and British Lieutenant General A. E. Percival, both of whom had previously surrendered to the Japanese.

U.S. ARMY PHOTOGRAPH

Index